BUTTERFLY BELIEVERS

BUTTERFLY BELIEVERS

PAUL E. LINZEY
Foreword by Eddie Espinosa

RESOURCE *Publications* · Eugene, Oregon

BUTTERFLY BELIEVERS

Copyright © 2023 Paul E. Linzey. All rights reserved. Except for brief quotations in critical publications or reviews, no part of this book may be reproduced in any manner without prior written permission from the publisher. Write: Permissions, Wipf and Stock Publishers, 199 W. 8th Ave., Suite 3, Eugene, OR 97401.

Resource Publications
An Imprint of Wipf and Stock Publishers
199 W. 8th Ave., Suite 3
Eugene, OR 97401

www.wipfandstock.com

PAPERBACK ISBN: 978-1-6667-7476-4
HARDCOVER ISBN: 978-1-6667-7477-1
EBOOK ISBN: 978-1-6667-7478-8

VERSION NUMBER 12/28/23

The sketch of the Monarch egg is from W. J. Holland's *The Butterfly Book*, which is in public domain. Other interior images are from pixabay.com and are used with permission.

Lyrics of the song *Change My Heart, O God* are used by permission from the composer, Eddie Espinosa.

All Scripture quotations, unless otherwise indicated, are taken from the Holy Bible, New International Version®, NIV®. Copyright ©1973, 1978, 1984, 2011 by Biblica, Inc.™ Used by permission of Zondervan. All rights reserved worldwide. www.zondervan.com. The "NIV" and "New International Version" are trademarks registered in the United States Patent and Trademark Office by Biblica, Inc.™

To Charlene Carr
Former Religious Education Director
at the United States Naval Academy

❦

Your investment in the lives of children, teens,
Midshipmen, and adults
Is the epitome of what it means to help others become
Butterfly Believers

I am grateful to have worked with you
And to be your friend

Contents

Foreword by Eddie Espinosa | ix
Introduction: Continuous Transformation | xi

Stage One: The Egg

Chapter 1 The Spiritual Journey Begins | 3
Chapter 2 Everything You Need | 5
Chapter 3 Room for Individuality | 8
Chapter 4 The Narrow Gate | 10
Chapter 5 Feeding the Mind | 12
Chapter 6 Single, Cluster, or Mass | 15
Chapter 7 Baby Steps | 17
Chapter 8 Make It to the Next Level | 20
Chapter 9 Time to Develop | 23
Chapter 10 Turn Up the Heat | 25
Chapter 11 Whatever It Takes | 29

Stage Two: The Caterpillar

Chapter 12 Inspiration | 35
Chapter 13 Creative Genius | 38
Chapter 14 One Head or Two | 41
Chapter 15 Built to Eat | 44
Chapter 16 Sensing the World | 48
Chapter 17 No Offense | 50
Chapter 18 We're Not Clones | 53
Chapter 19 Ornaments | 56

Chapter 20	It's a War Out There | 59
Chapter 21	Friendship and Fellowship | 63
Chapter 22	Personal Assessment | 66
Chapter 23	Time Out | 69
Chapter 24	Are We There Yet | 71

Stage Three: The Chrysalis

Chapter 25	Foundational Attachments | 77
Chapter 26	Appreciating Our Differences | 79
Chapter 27	What's on the Inside | 81
Chapter 28	Transformation | 84
Chapter 29	Magic or Miracle | 87

Stage Four: The Imago

Chapter 30	Going Through the Fire | 93
Chapter 31	Restoring the Beauty | 96
Chapter 32	Design and Destiny | 99
Chapter 33	Disciple and Discipler | 101
Chapter 34	Pollinators | 103
Chapter 35	More Than Meets the Eye | 106
Chapter 36	X-Ray Vision | 108
Chapter 37	Malformations | 110
Chapter 38	Natural Interests | 113
Chapter 39	Living Up to Our Potential | 116
Chapter 40	*Butterfly Believers* | 119

How to Lead a Discussion Group or Class \| 123
One Anothers of the New Testament \| 126
About the Author \| 128
Books by Paul E. Linzey \| 130
The Music and Ministry of Eddie Espinosa \| 131
Bibliography \| 133
Scripture Index \| 137

Foreword

I WAS A LITTLE more than two weeks away from my sixteenth birthday when I prayed what so many have called "the sinner's prayer." I didn't know exactly what had happened to me, but one thing for sure . . . I was a different person. I felt different, I acted differently, and I thought differently. I couldn't explain it, but I knew something great had happened. I knew that my sins had been forgiven because of what the Lord Jesus Christ had accomplished on the cross. I was as light as a feather.

At that young age, it could be said that I hadn't accumulated a ton of sins, but there was one trait that all of my friends knew me very well for. I could cuss up a storm like any well-traveled, island-hopping sailor, or perhaps like the leader of a ruthless motorcycle gang. I'd mention rapper or aging rock star, but the year was 1969 and there was very little exposure to "cussing." After all, movies and television shows were censored and monitored for inappropriate language. Nonetheless, I used profanity in place of adjectives in my daily conversations. That was the first thing to go. A transformation had begun, and it seemed effortless!

I suddenly had a voracious appetite for the Word of God and began memorizing Scripture in order to "keep my way pure." All my friends noticed the difference. I was off to a great start. Then it happened!!! I slammed the car door on my finger and out it came. My first major transgression that I thought I had under control. It had been weeks, maybe months, since that glorious day. I remember thinking, "Did I just lose my salvation? Does God hate

Foreword

me now? How do I get back on track? I'm sure you've never experienced this . . . or have you?

In this wonderful new book, Paul Linzey has captured what growing and walking with Christ is all about. He has written forty captivating devotional "reads" that are like a mesmerizing script of a nature channel documentary. He beautifully describes metamorphosis in the natural, expertly shows us the Biblical reality of what happens in our lives, and exquisitely depicts exactly what believers all over the world have experienced for centuries.

As you read, you will learn so much more about the beautiful creatures that we so often overlook simply because, unlike butterflies, we don't stop to smell the roses, much less place ourselves in an environment where we can be still and know that the Creator of butterflies, who also created us, has given us all that we need to grow. His desire is for us to be molded and shaped into the image of Christ, that we might reflect His glory.

God often speaks to us through his creation, of which butterflies are among the most beautiful. After reading this great book, I will never see butterflies in the same way. I'm encouraged by a new metamorphosis in me.

When our children were young, we bought a vinyl copy of a popular Christian children's musical at the time called "Bullfrogs and Butterflies." The composers did a magnificent job of teaching children how like "bullfrogs and butterflies, we've all been born again." Like the catchy tune and lyrics of those songs taught our children about the work of the cross, *Butterfly Believers* is for believers of all ages, and trust me, we're never too old to learn.

Eddie Espinosa, Composer
Change My Heart, O God

Introduction

Continuous Transformation

WHILE PREACHING THROUGH THE New Testament book of Romans, I came to chapter twelve, verse two, and quickly realized the significance of the word "transformed." The word in the Greek New Testament is μεταμορφουσθε (metamorphousthe), a word that comes into English as "metamorphosis." Further research led me to a lifelong love for butterflies.

> *Therefore, I urge you, brothers and sisters, in view of God's mercy, to offer your bodies as a living sacrifice, holy and pleasing to God—this is your true and proper worship. Do not conform to the pattern of this world, but be transformed by the renewing of your mind. Then you will be able to test and approve what God's will is—his good, pleasing and perfect will* (Romans 12:1–2).

There are many ways to discuss discipleship, what it takes to grow spiritually, and how to become the people we are meant to be, but the metamorphosis of butterflies may provide the best analogy because the changes are drastic and visible, as are many of the changes that take place when we come to Christ. The

xi

Continuous Transformation

metamorphic process results in beauty and maturity, and the Lord wants to develop both of these traits in our lives.

Several insects undergo complete metamorphosis, including bees, ants, ladybugs, wasps, and flies. But the most spectacular of the metamorphosing creatures are the butterflies and moths. This is because they are safe, easy to observe, and many of them are beautiful. Ever since that study in Romans and my personal discovery of metamorphosis, I've loved butterflies. I've read about them and have visited butterfly houses, exhibits, gardens, parks, pavilions, and encounters around the country. My wife and I have a butterfly garden at our home and joined the North American Butterfly Association as well as the Missouri Botanical Gardens.

Amazingly, transformation occurs in every stage of the butterfly's life. There is never a day when an egg, caterpillar, chrysalis, or butterfly is the same as it was the day before. Theirs is literally a continuous transformation. This is also true of people. We are always growing, changing, and becoming. There's always more to learn, and always room for refinement.

For several years, I've wanted to write a book on spiritual growth using metamorphosis as a model for how we change throughout a lifetime. When Pastor Steve Elliot asked my wife and me to speak at the United Methodist South Seaville Camp Meeting,[1] and then he selected "transformation" as the theme, I knew immediately that this was the time to write this book.

Butterflies are special to me for several reasons. First is the fact that they represent the internal and external changes that take place when a person comes to faith in Jesus Christ. Second is the mystery, or as some writers call it, the "magic" of the changes that occur during the transformation process. Third is the gorgeous coloration of so many species. They are delightful to find and examine.

The bottom line is that I find butterflies to be interesting and fun. In the same way, living for Jesus Christ is interesting and fun. Many of the terms and processes we use when talking about butterflies are perfect for discussing our growth as children of God.

1. United Methodists of Greater New Jersey, Cape Atlantic District.

Continuous Transformation

The bibliography presents several books and articles that provide additional information for those who want to go deeper. In addition, there are many websites where you can take a look at some awesome pictures of these marvelous creatures called *Lepidoptera*, which means scaly wings.

The four stages of the butterfly life cycle provide an easy way to organize this book, and in each stage, there are some fascinating changes. After a brief description of one aspect of the butterfly, I will introduce a verse or two from the Bible that talk about the potential for growth in our lives.

Music has always been an important part of my life, and whenever I prepare a sermon or Bible study, a specific song will play in my mind. Usually, it's a worship song with lyrics that coincide with the scripture and the theme I'm writing about. In this case, from the moment I began thinking about the transformation we experience as believers, the tune that kept recurring in my mind was one of my all-time favorite worship songs: *Change My Heart, O God* by Eddie Espinosa.

I don't know how many times I've gone over to the piano to sing that song, worship the Lord, and make the message of the lyrics the prayer of my own heart. That's why I am particularly thankful that Eddie agreed to write the foreword for this book.

Whether you're reading this by yourself or with a discussion group with a few friends, my hope is that you enjoy Christianity as much as I do, and that you will continue growing *in the grace and knowledge of our Lord and Savior, Jesus Christ until the day we see him face to face.*[2]

While reading this book, perhaps you'll learn something new about butterflies and living for Christ. And maybe gain some insight into yourself, too. So sit back, relax, and get ready for forty devotional readings about butterflies and spirituality.

Your Friend and Fellow Butterfly Believer,
Paul Linzey

---

2. 2 Peter 3:18

STAGE ONE

The Egg

Egg of a Monarch Butterfly
(enlarged)

CHAPTER 1

The Spiritual Journey Begins

WHEN DISCUSSING PLANTS AND animals, a fundamental principle of modern science is that every living thing comes from an egg, and this is where our story about *Butterfly Believers* begins. After mating, a female butterfly deposits her eggs on or under a leaf, gluing it on so that it cannot be blown off or removed.

The outer layer of the egg itself is a hard membrane called a chorion, which protects the caterpillar embryo. The chorion has thousands of microscopic pores that allow the embryo to breathe while inside the egg.[1] In many species, the caterpillar hatches in just a few days.

Every one of us begins the spiritual journey somewhere. We might have grown up in a Christian family. Some are invited to a church or a small group that meets in a home. Others come to faith in Christ later in life. Whoever we are and wherever we find ourselves spiritually, the Lord reaches out to us and provides the spark of faith, fans it into flame, and our walk of faith begins.

---

1. wisconsinpollinators.com

This can be seen in my own family. My grandfather converted to Christ at about age seventy-five, living the last twenty-four years of his life as a dedicated Christian who read the scriptures every day and became a deacon in the little Baptist church near his farm. My father was a sailor in the Navy when he met a young lady who invited him to church. He became a Christian and they eventually married. That's why I grew up in a Christian home.

I know people who turned to God during a crisis and found that the Lord provided the help they needed. I've talked with others who just felt there was something missing in their life and discovered a God who filled the emptiness inside. A few have told me they had a friend who changed so much after experiencing Christ that they were drawn to the Lord. There are others who came to faith because of a miraculous experience.

The Lord might use people in our lives to help us grow. We see this in 1 Corinthians 3:5–7, where the writer uses a different metaphor.

> *What, after all, is Apollos? And what is Paul? Only servants, through whom you came to believe—as the Lord has assigned to each his task. I planted the seed, Apollos watered it, but God has been making it grow. So neither the one who plants nor the one who waters is anything, but only God, who makes things grow.*

In these verses, the Corinthian believers are likened to a plant or a crop. Their faith journey began when someone planted the seed. The Lord sent someone else to provide the water. The seeds sprouted, took root, began to grow, and then flourished.

The point is that we all have to start somewhere. In the same way that every plant or animal comes from an egg, each of us begins the spiritual journey like that butterfly egg. We are alive. We have potential. The Lord wants to take us step by step on a path that will help us develop emotionally, relationally, and spiritually.

Chapter 2

Everything You Need

WHEN THE FEMALE BUTTERFLY places an egg on the leaf, it contains the yolk: a thick liquid that has the "germ" of the future caterpillar plus the food it will need until it hatches. This is crucial because even though the critter might be in the egg for only a week or two, it requires immediate nourishment or it will die.

This is one of many details about the butterfly life cycle that provides what some would consider to be "a stunning display of evolutionary mechanism at work,"[1] or what others would see as an amazing demonstration of the brilliance of the creator. Either way, it is fascinating that in every step of the metamorphic process, there is a marvelous combination of beauty and function.

I think this is also true for human beings, especially in the context of the quest for spiritual growth. When we start our journey as a disciple, everything we need to sustain our new life of faith is in place. We have the Holy Spirit living inside of us. We have a sense of faith, even if it's at the embryonic level. These two will sustainment us and carry us to the next level.

1. Puiu, "How Butterflies Gruesomely Transform into Butterflies."

Stage One | The Egg

Peter tells us in 2 Peter 1:3-4:

> *His divine power has given us everything we need for a godly life through our knowledge of him who called us by his own glory and goodness. Through these he has given us his very great and precious promises, so that through them you may participate in the divine nature, having escaped the corruption in the world caused by evil desires.*

In the passage above, do you notice the goal of participating in the divine nature? That will be the focal point when we get to the discussion of the adult butterfly. The creature still in the egg isn't even close to looking like or behaving like the mature insect. It's not even a crawling bug yet. There are many changes that will have to happen before it gets to the finish line.

Similarly, there are many changes and much growth a believer has to experience before getting to where the Lord wants him or her to be. So, we take it one day at a time until we see the Lord's handiwork manifesting in our life and character.

Years ago, there was a guest minister speaking at our church. In his presentation, it was evident that he knew the scriptures. Regardless of the topic, he understood what the Word of God had to say about it and how it could be applied in the life of the church as well as in the individual believer. Listening to him speak, two thoughts went through my mind. First, I was impressed at the way he handled various topics biblically. Second, I felt shame that even though I had been a practicing Christian for quite a while, I didn't know the Bible very well. While sitting there in church, I prayed that the Lord would help me learn the scriptures better, and that very week I started reading and studying a bit more faithfully.

Six years later, I was in a Bible study group when a complicated issue came up for discussion. Someone asked me what I thought about it. After I gave an answer, one of the men in the group said, "Wow, I wish I knew the Bible as well as you do, and understood how to apply it in day-to-day life." Right then, I remembered my experience and prayer from six years prior and thanked the Lord for helping me grow.

Everything You Need

There's nothing wrong with being in the egg if you're brand new to the life of faith or haven't even started yet. It's totally fine to be where you are at this stage of your spiritual life. Take nourishment from what's around you, learn from others, and ask the Lord for his help. I guarantee that his divine power will give you everything you need for a godly life, and if you hang in there, you are well on your way to participating in the divine nature. That's God's promise . . . even for those who are still in the egg.

Chapter 3

Room for Individuality

I USED TO ASSUME that all butterfly eggs were identical regardless of the species. Maybe some were slightly smaller and some a bit bigger, but otherwise, one butterfly egg would be just like every other butterfly egg. Oh, how wrong I was! When I started investigating, I discovered that the eggs of different types of butterflies are sometimes quite different from every other kind.

Some are round and others hemispherical. Some are conical, cylindrical, or shaped like a barrel. Some resemble a cheese wheel, while others actually look like a turban. Many butterfly eggs are angular, and many appear to be flattened at the ends. There's a wide variety of textures, sizes, designs, and colors.[1] There are blues, reds, greens, yellows, purples, oranges, whites, and browns. Oh, my goodness, there are some fascinating differences among them!

The same is true among human beings, and even among Christians of similar theology or the same denomination. We have different personalities, talents, and preferences. We don't have the same spiritual gifts, callings, or interests. We definitely don't look

---

1. Holland, *The Butterfly Book*, 4.

Room for Individuality

alike. We don't agree on every doctrine, type of music, or choice of liturgy. In addition, there are many different relationship styles among us. Who we are and what we are like depends so much on our genetics, our upbringing, our experiences, our health, and so much more.

The Apostle Paul takes this into account when he discusses the Gifts of the Spirit.

> *Just as a body, though one, has many parts, but all its many parts form one body, so it is with Christ. There are many parts, but one body. 1 Corinthians 12:12, 20.*

Another take on the differences among the people of God can be seen in Galatians 3:28. *There is neither Jew nor Gentile, neither slave nor free, nor is there male and female, for you are all one in Christ Jesus.*

It's important to keep in mind that the differences among us are good. We shouldn't try to be like one another, nor should we try to force others to be like us. In fact, there is greater health in our fellowship and friendship circles when we invite diversity into the mix.

A *Butterfly Believer* in the egg or embryo stage might want to keep in mind that even though there may be some important changes ahead, you don't have to become just like everyone else. There's plenty of room for individuality. You can still be you. A better aim for all of us would be to give each other space to grow into the likeness and the image of the Lord. That's what we were created for.

Chapter 4

The Narrow Gate

THE EXTERIOR OF A butterfly egg has at least one tiny opening called a *micropyle*, while the egg of a different species may have an entire "system of tiny canals."[1] These microscopic openings permit the entrance of the sperm, so that the egg may be fertilized shortly before it is deposited by the female. Interestingly, *micropyle* is the transliteration of a Greek compound word meaning "little doors" or "little gates." Both plant and insect eggs have these miniature openings. Otherwise, there would be no fertilization.

It's true that Jesus mentioned moths and gnats in his teaching, but I don't know whether he ever talked about their eggs. On the other hand, he did talk about doors and gates. In fact, he specifically mentioned a small gate in the Sermon on the Mount:

> Enter through the narrow gate. For wide is the gate and broad is the road that leads to destruction, and many enter through it. But small is the gate and narrow the road that leads to life, and only a few find it (Mat 7:13-14).

---

1. Culin, "Lepidopteran," *Britannica*.

This verse uses the same word for gate, door, or opening that is used to discuss plant and insect eggs. The Septuagint uses the same word in Psalm 118:19, *Open for me the gates of the righteous; I will enter and give thanks to the Lord.*

Later on, Jesus made this statement, *I am the gate; whoever enters through me will be saved* (John 10:9).

Perhaps there's one other scripture that ought to be included in this discussion. *Behold, I stand at the door, and knock: if anyone hears my voice, opens the door, and welcomes me in, I will come in and fellowship* (Revelation 3:20, paraphrased). This is a specific invitation for *Butterfly Believers* who are looking for spiritual direction and fulfillment.

A friend of mine has a saying: "Christianity isn't a religion; it's a relationship." I like that emphasis because it captures the essence of what Jesus is all about. Living for Christ is not about liturgy, ritual, traditions, or rules, even though many of those might be good and helpful. I've discovered that genuine Christianity involves growing a deep relationship with the Savior who calls himself our friend.

Chapter 5

Feeding the Mind

THE FEMALE BUTTERFLY INSTINCTIVELY knows that her hatchlings are limited as to what kind of plant they will eat, and places her eggs only on that plant. Therefore, when it's time to lay the eggs, the mother-to-be searches for the appropriate host plant for her youngsters to grow up on. "She finds these by sight and smell, landing on a plant of choice and scratching the leaf surface to 'taste' it with her feet."[1]

When the caterpillars emerge from the eggs, many of them eat the shell of the egg first, and then proceed to live the rest of their lives on that particular host plant. People who want to attract certain kinds of butterflies will do a little research to find out what that breed will eat, because the egg-laying butterfly won't be fooled. For example, a Monarch eats only milkweed. A Viceroy has a few options: willow, poplar, aspen, apple, cherry, or plum. The Zebra Swallowtail needs pawpaw. And the Pearl Crescent is

---

1. Burris, *The Life Cycles of Butterflies*, 3.

Feeding the Mind

limited to asters.[2] The list goes on and on, and is particular to each variety of butterfly.

Because the context for this entire discussion is Romans 12:1–2, it may be helpful to understand that we are instructed not to *conform to the pattern of this world, but be transformed by the renewing of your mind*. According to the extended metaphor of metamorphosis, the food we're concerned about is what we're feeding our minds, because that's the issue at stake in this verse and in our day-to-day lives. Therefore, it's crucial that we select the appropriate "host plant" for our mind and spirit.

The kind of *Butterfly Believer* you are will determine what you feed on, where you spend your time, what you read, who you hang out with, and what you choose for entertainment. A few relevant questions include: "Who and what are you allowing to influence you?" "Are your choices helping you to be strong in your faith and more faithful as a follower of Christ?" "Are you developing a keen sense of discernment, or like the butterflies, a well-developed instinctive knowing what is right or wrong when it comes to feeding?"

The apostle Paul wrote to one congregation:

> *Finally, brothers and sisters, whatever is true, whatever is noble, whatever is right, whatever is pure, whatever is lovely, whatever is admirable—if anything is excellent or praiseworthy—think about such things* (Philippians 4:8).

Being in Iraq during the war provided some personal difficulties for just about everyone who was there, including me. It was dangerous and scary, and I experienced real fear. Being away from home for a long time meant there were sexual temptations. We had quite a few casualties, and everyone lived with severe stress. A lot of people relied on eating comfort food and gained weight. Others turned to alcohol or drugs.

> A lot of people think, when they're that far from home and the circumstances are that bad, that they are justified in doing things they wouldn't do otherwise. But instead

2. Kelly, "What Do Caterpillars Eat?"

Stage One | The Egg

of giving in to the temptations and the opportunities for sex, drugs, or porn, I spent time with other Christian men, listened to Christian music, and worked out at the gym. I ate pecan pie a la mode and oatmeal raisin cookies. I read my Bible and anything decent I could get my hands on. I prayed with some of the men who came to church or to one of the Bible studies. And, I called home as often as I could.[3]

There is no "one size fits all" approach. What you do to care for and feed your mind and your spirit is extremely important, but also highly personal. Like the butterfly that looks for the right host plant to land on, you have to discover what works for you. And yet, you can also learn from others. As it says in Philippians 4:9, *Whatever you have learned or received or heard from me, or seen in me—put it into practice. And the God of peace will be with you*

---

3. Linzey, *Safest Place in Iraq*, 73.

CHAPTER 6

Single, Cluster, or Mass

THE AVERAGE FEMALE WILL deposit from one hundred to three hundred eggs, some will produce as few as a dozen, and others more than a thousand. Some butterflies will place the eggs on the leaf one at a time. Others will deposit a group or a cluster of eggs. Some will stack them neatly, one on top of another. Still others will release a mass of eggs in a pile. Whatever method the female butterfly uses, she will glue them onto the leaf, stem, flower, seedpod, or tendril to make sure they won't come off. The glue is so strong that it's impossible to remove the egg without destroying the creature inside.

There are two similarities to *Butterfly Believers* I'd like to point out here. First, in the same way some eggs are laid one at a time and others are piled or grouped in a mass, some people come to faith in Christ individually while others are part of a large gathering where there may be hundreds who respond to the gospel at the same time.

I met one man who dreamed that he met Jesus. That dream led him to "count the cost" and commit his life to Christ, even

Stage One | The Egg

though he lived in a place where there was serious persecution. The expression "count the cost" comes from Luke 14:28, where Jesus said to a large crowd:

> *For which of you, intending to build a tower, does not sit down first and count the cost, whether he has enough to finish it?* Later, when talking to his disciples, he told them, *Whoever wants to be my disciple must deny the self, take up his or her cross and follow me* (Matthew 16:24).

I was six years old when my mother took our family to a camp meeting in a revival tent. Listening to the preacher, I understood for the first time that Jesus went to the cross for my sins. I turned to my brother and said, "I'm going up to get saved," and he replied, "Me too!" We ran up the center aisle, around to the wooden benches behind the platform, and knelt until someone came and prayed with us. I don't remember if there was anyone else praying to receive Christ as Lord and Savior that night, but there were at least two of us.

Years later, I attended several Billy Graham rallies in huge stadiums. When Dr. Graham gave a salvation altar call, literally hundreds of people left their seats, found their way to the ball field below, and *en masse*, committed their lives to Jesus Christ. It was an individual decision each person had to make, but it happened in a much larger setting than my boyhood experience or the man who had the dream.

The second similarity has to do with the church or fellowship we might choose to attend. Some people live in a place where there is no church or congregation, so they worship, read the scriptures, and pray all by themselves. Many people around the world attend small churches of anywhere from ten people to fifty or sixty. And a lot of people prefer what we call a megachurch, which may have hundreds or even thousands gathering at the same time and place.

Again, there are many ways to come to Christ, and many approaches to participating in the body of Christ. Size really isn't the point. What matters is devotion to Christ, growing in your faith, and recognizing that you are part of the family of God.

Chapter 7

Baby Steps

Whenever I take on a new activity, start playing a new game, or dig into researching a new topic, my natural desire is that I want to be good at it immediately. This is true whether playing Settlers of Catan the first time, taking trumpet lessons as a kid, or deciding later in life to get seriously into table tennis. The problem is that learning any new skill, art, or body of knowledge takes time, even for those who seem to be naturally gifted. Some people pick up new skills rather quickly, while others take a bit longer.

This dynamic plays out at our house over and over again. We'll hear about a new game from our kids or friends; we'll buy the game and start playing it; my wife will catch on really fast and win the game every single time we play; I get discouraged and never want to play it again. But then I begin to understand the strategies and start winning once in a while.

The same may be true for *Butterfly Believers*. When we're just getting started in the life of faith, we might not be very good at it yet. We continue in some of our old ways, making a few too many errors, and then we get discouraged and want to quit. But don't

Stage One | The Egg

give up, and don't throw in the towel just yet, my friend. There's hope for you. The goal at the start is to be a good egg. Being a good caterpillar will happen later. Eventually, you'll have a chance to be a great butterfly.

The first noticeable change that happens to an egg is that a few days after being deposited, it starts to change color.

> Many eggs start out light colored like an off-white to a yellow color then change to a dark color or black before the caterpillar comes out. Most caterpillars hatch out of the eggs in 3–7 days. It can vary depending on species and other conditions.[1]

Green or blue eggs may also turn gradually darker, and if you were to look at the eggs through a microscope at just the right time, you'd be able to see the tiny caterpillars starting to develop.[2]

The butterfly life cycle is one of complete transformation . . . in every stage . . . in every part of every stage . . . all the way to the end of its existence. It never stays the same. It's always changing in some way. Sometimes the changes are easily observable. But sometimes you might not even know the change is happening because it's subtle . . . or invisible.

This is helpful for us to keep in mind as disciples of Jesus Christ in the process of becoming who we are meant to be. Change takes time. Learning is incremental. Like Bill Murray's character in the movie *What About Bob*, we start a new endeavor or life skill by taking baby steps. Another character of his was the weatherman in *Groundhog Day*, who lived the same day over and over and over, until he finally learned what he needed to know in order to become the person he needed to be.

So hang in there. Don't give up the faith or let go of your commitment to Christ. Don't quit the church. It may be that the changes are happening at the invisible level right now, and in just a few days you'll be ready to hatch and become a caterpillar. And then a whole new existence begins.

1. Kelly, "How to Find Butterfly Eggs."
2. Holland, *The Butterfly Book*, 5.

Baby Steps

As the apostle writes in 2 Corinthians 3:18, *We all are being transformed into his image with ever-increasing glory.*

Chapter 8

Make It to the Next Level

"Of the few hundred butterfly eggs laid, very few will reach adulthood,"[1] and there are a lot of reasons for this. Even though the eggs are glued securely to the plant, they are quite vulnerable. If the weather is too cold or too dry, they won't survive. They are often eaten by birds, snails, spiders, other insects, and reptiles. Grazing animals sometimes eat the leaves the eggs were laid on.

One of the worst problems is that microscopic wasps get into the butterfly eggs and eat the yolk.[2] Sometimes, the eggs are laid never having been fertilized. When this happens, the eggs will dry out and rot. As you can see, there are many dangers awaiting the butterfly eggs, which is why the vast majority will not survive and make it to the next stage. Who knew?

But butterfly eggs aren't the only creatures whose survival is in jeopardy. Baby Christians will also experience perilous times. Peter tells us to *Be alert and of sober mind. Your enemy the devil prowls around like a roaring lion looking for someone to devour* (1

---

1. Johnson, "Facts About Butterfly Eggs," *Sciencing*.
2. Pavid, "Body Snatchers," *Natural History Museum*.

Peter 5:8). Paul writes in his letter to Timothy that many will fall into temptations and traps *that plunge people into ruin and destruction* (1 Timothy 6:9). Perhaps the Lord himself described it best in his Parable of the Sower and the Seed.

> *Listen then to what the parable of the sower means: When anyone hears the message about the kingdom and does not understand it, the evil one comes and snatches away what was sown in their heart. This is the seed sown along the path. The seed falling on rocky ground refers to someone who hears the word and at once receives it with joy. But since they have no root, they last only a short time. When trouble or persecution comes because of the word, they quickly fall away. The seed falling among the thorns refers to someone who hears the word, but the worries of this life and the deceitfulness of wealth choke the word, making it unfruitful. But the seed falling on good soil refers to someone who hears the word and understands it. This is the one who produces a crop, yielding a hundred, sixty or thirty times what was sown.* (Matthew 13:1–23).

In the same way that butterfly eggs have a tough time making it to the next level, *Butterfly Believers* also have a tough time surviving temptations, distractions, the devil, the cares and concerns of life, deception, lack of depth, or having no roots. St. Paul would add false teachers and persecution to the list. Hebrews would suggest that there are sins that entangle us and may jeopardize our walk with the Lord.

On the other hand, there is a purpose in our struggles. James reminds us to *Consider it pure joy, my brothers and sisters, whenever you face trials of many kinds, because you know that the testing of your faith produces perseverance. Let perseverance finish its work so that you may be mature and complete, not lacking anything* (James 1:2–4).

Mature and complete. Not lacking anything. Strong enough to endure whatever we face. That's what the Lord has in mind for us. He has given us his spirit for strength, guidance, and inspiration. He also places people in our lives to encourage and mentor us. We have what it takes to make it. No wonder James can tell us to be joyful. But we still have to go through the storms and struggles.

This is what the people of God experienced during the tough days after they returned from the Babylonian captivity and started rebuilding the walls of Jerusalem. They faced all sorts of difficulties. Yet, Nehemiah could stand up and proclaim to the people, *The joy of the Lord is your strength* (Nehemiah 8:10). And he was right.

Chapter 9

Time to Develop

In warm, tropical areas of the earth, a caterpillar might emerge from the egg just two days after it was placed on the host plant, but in the colder, northern parts of the world, such as in the Arctic regions, the eggs might hibernate or lie dormant all winter long, which means the caterpillar will stay inside 3–6 months before breaking free and continuing the process of becoming a butterfly.

The variations of time largely have to do with the temperature. But if it survives, whether a caterpillar was in the egg 3 days, 3 weeks, or 3 months, the end result is the same. A voraciously hungry caterpillar bites and claws its way out and starts eating whatever suitable vegetation it can find so it can build up the bulk and stamina it's going to need later on.

There's an important lesson here for *Butterfly Believers* who live in an era of instant gratification. When we want something, we usually want it right now. But spiritual growth takes time. Personal maturity requires many years. Building a lasting relationship, whether with another person or with God, doesn't happen instantly. So we have to be patient, persistent, and faithful.

Stage One | The Egg

Every college football player has the dream of getting into the NFL and being a smashing success right from the beginning of the rookie year: starting every game, being in the playoffs, winning the championship, making big money, receiving the MVP trophy, everything. The reality is that it takes most players several years to reach their peak. After years of working hard, maybe with a couple of injuries and failures, they finally get to the place of consistent, high-level performance . . . if they last long enough in the league.

The same is true in our walk with the Lord. We have high hopes. We want to be mature and spiritually deep. We feel an urgency to participate in ministry. But the sometimes-painful truth is that we might not be ready for that yet, which is why James said *Not many of you should become teachers* (James 3:1) and Paul wrote that a leader in the Kingdom of God *must not be a recent convert* (1 Timothy 3:6).

There's another reason for being patient. When we try to rush the process, we tend to set ourselves up for failure or disillusionment, and this can be devastating, leading many to drop out of church or give up the faith entirely.

In the same way caterpillars have to be patient and hatch at the right time, and just like athletes have to develop skills over time and earn a starting spot on the team, *Butterfly Believers* will focus on the Lord, allow spiritually mature brothers and sisters to provide discipleship and mentoring, not pretend to be more mature than they really are, and not try to take on leadership responsibilities too soon. The end result will be better for the individuals and for the congregation. And most assuredly, they'll end up with a much better win-loss record than if they tried to rush into starting positions. As the proverb reminds us:

> *Trust in the Lord with all your heart and lean not on your own understanding; in all your ways submit to him, and he will make your paths straight* (Proverbs 3:5–6).

Chapter 10

Turn Up the Heat

During the summer of 2012, the NBC television station in Albany, New York, reported that "the Karner Blue Butterfly produced an unprecedented third generation this year thanks to an early start on mating."[1] Every year, there are precisely two broods of the rare Karner Blue, but newscasters referenced an Associated Press article that said there were three generations that year. The reason? It was a warmer-than-average spring, which led to earlier-than-usual mating.

> Neil Gifford, conservation director of the Albany Pine Bush Preserve, has been working for 16 seasons to preserve the federally endangered butterfly, which lives on spring-blooming lupines. The impact of the third brood on the insect's population depends on whether there are enough lupines left to feed the caterpillars.[2]

One complete cycle from egg to maturity is called a brood, and many butterflies have only one brood per year. In the warmer

---

1. "Warmer weather begets more butterfly broods." *NBC5*.
2. Ibid.

Stage One | The Egg

areas of the earth, there may be as many as three broods each year, and in the far north, some butterflies "need 2 summers to complete one brood."[3] But in the tropics, there are butterflies with four or five generations and at least one species with as many as eight.[4]

The idea that butterfly reproduction and growth are related to the temperature surprised me at first, but it makes sense. According to Hilaire Ashworth at the Lewis Botanical Garden in Richmond, Virginia, "Butterflies can't even fly if their body temperature is less than 86 degrees Fahrenheit! Butterflies are cold blooded."[5] They get their heat from basking in the sun, their large wings taking in the heat like solar panels.

Have you ever heard the expression that someone was *on fire*? It's used similarly in several contexts. For example, if a basketball player is scoring more points than he usually does and isn't missing any shots, the announcer might say, "He's on fire!" This was popularized by the video game *NBA JAM* in the 1990s.[6] If a corporate executive makes a series of important organizational or product decisions that leads her corporation to explode in sales and revenue, a business analyst might write "She's on fire!"

A similar comment can be made when a *Butterfly Believer* is growing spiritually, engaging in the spiritual disciplines, and feeling particularly close to God. An observer in the church or in the family might say "She's on fire for God."

It's pretty common for new converts to be on fire for the Lord because they're excited about their new life in Christ. The feelings of forgiveness and freedom are wonderful and there's so much to learn and do in this new life. It's also pretty common for the flame to gradually cool off. I heard a pair of "mature saints" talking about a new Christian who started attending their church. The conversation went something like this:

"Wow! He sure is on fire!"

"I know! I remember when I used to be like that."

3. "Life Cycle." *Nature North*.
4. Clarke, "All-female broods in the butterfly Hypolimnas bolina (L.)."
5. Ashworth, "Butterflies: Warming Up."
6. Myres, "The Behind-the-Scenes Story of 'He's On Fire!' in NBA Jam."

Turn Up the Heat

"How long do you think it'll last."

"Give him time. It'll wear off, and he'll be like the rest of us."

That is such a sad comment on the spiritual condition of too many Christians. While it may be true that none of us can live in a state of spiritual excitement all the time, there is a danger of getting too cold spiritually, to the point where we are no longer productive, active, or even alive. A butterfly that is too cold for too long will die. The same is true for a *Butterfly Believer*.

There's an interesting comment in Revelation chapter three, in the Letter to the Church in Laodicea, about the relative heat of the people in the church.

> *These are the words of the Amen, the faithful and true witness, the ruler of God's creation. I know your deeds, that you are neither cold nor hot. I wish you were either one or the other! So, because you are lukewarm—neither hot nor cold—I am about to spit you out of my mouth* (Revelation 3:14–16).

The fact is, we can live in the light of God's glory, and we can be on fire spiritually, enjoying a wonderful sense of the presence of God and the Power of God in our day-to-day lives. The Lord doesn't want us to feel distant from him. And we don't have to! Like the butterfly that needs to bask in the sunlight to absorb its heat, we can bask in the presence of the Son of God and absorb the warmth of his love and his goodness.

But what if the butterfly is too cold to even get to a place in the sun? Interestingly, there is something a butterfly can do to get just enough of the juices flowing to start moving.

Besides basking, butterflies take part in another behavioral strategy called shivering. This is exactly what it sounds like. Butterflies will rapidly shake or shiver in order to raise their body temperatures to prepare for flight. This heats up the thorax (abdomen) and helps them fly a short distance.[7]

---

7. Ashworth, "Butterflies: Warming Up."

Stage One | The Egg

MercyMe is a contemporary Christian group that has a song called "Shake." The song talks about being transformed, changed, and brought back to life. Here are a couple of lines from the lyrics:

> *You gotta shake, shake, shake,*
> *Like you're changed, changed, changed*
> *Brand new looks so good on you,*
> *So shake like you've been changed*

If you find yourself a bit colder spiritually than you want to be, maybe it's time to shake. Shake off the doldrums, move to a place where you can spend some time in the sun . . . or with the Son . . . and allow the warmth of the presence of God to revive and rekindle your faith. The same Letter to the Church in Laodicea concludes with this promise.

> *To the one who is victorious, I will give the right to sit with me on my throne, just as I was victorious and sat down with my Father on his throne* (Revelation 3:21).

Maybe it's time to turn up the heat.

Chapter 11

Whatever It Takes

WHEN THE TIME IS right, the caterpillar is ready to hatch and emerge from the egg. For many lepidopterans (the order of insects consisting of butterflies and moths), this occurs just two or three days after the female lays the eggs. But there are some that won't hatch until after more than a week, sometimes two. The exact moment is determined by the size of the caterpillar growing in the egg. When the individual grows to the egg's maximum capacity, the egg will crack. In some eggs, there's a "cap" that breaks off. In many cases, the caterpillar helps the process by cutting, clawing, or biting through the shell until it is able to wiggle out.

This is a significant point for *Butterfly Believers* who want to do what it takes to get to the next stage, because it's not going to happen without some effort. Growth is not automatic. There are times you might have to "bite, scratch, and claw" in order to survive. Not literally, of course, but in terms of being willing to do what it takes to get out of your shell, get to where you need to be, and keep on growing.

Stage One | The Egg

One suggestion might be to take a spiritual health assessment or do a spiritual growth analysis in order to become fully aware of your own needs. You might consider talking to a minister, Bible teacher, a small group leader, or a spiritually mature friend to get some guidance before doing this.

We all have needs, and the needs sometimes differ depending on our circumstances. For example, people with children might need to be in a church that has a good children's ministry. Some people are highly affected by music and may require a well-developed worship and music program. Others are more needy in terms of the content of the preaching and teaching. And still others have reached the place where they should be serving in ministry, no longer merely spectating.

Remember, butterfly metamorphosis is continuous. The critter is never the same from one day to the next, and the same is true for *Butterfly Believers*. We are designed to grow, to change, to be in the process of becoming what the Lord wants us to be.

I heard one man give this testimony: "I'm not yet what I'm gonna be, but thank God I'm not what I used to be." I like that because it includes the recognition that even though he isn't perfect, at least he is moving in the right direction. That's all the Lord asks of us whatever stage we happen to be in.

In his letter to friends who met for worship at the home of a woman named Lydia, St. Paul discusses his own commitment to doing what it takes to keep on growing spiritually and continue moving closer to the Lord Jesus Christ:

> *I want to know Christ—yes, to know the power of his resurrection and participation in his sufferings, becoming like him in his death, and so, somehow, attaining to the resurrection from the dead. Not that I have already obtained all this, or have already arrived at my goal, but I press on to take hold of that for which Christ Jesus took hold of me. Brothers and sisters, I do not consider myself yet to have taken hold of it. But one thing I do: Forgetting what is behind and straining toward what is ahead, I press on toward the goal to win the prize for which God has called me heavenward in Christ Jesus* (Philippians 3:10–14).

This passage is worth re-reading, and perhaps memorizing, because it captures the apostolic commitment to a personal relationship with Jesus Christ and doing whatever it takes to make that happen. The caterpillar instinctively knows it cannot remain in the egg. It has to get out so it can begin the next stage of its existence. What do you need to do to keep moving in the direction God has designed for you?

STAGE TWO

The Caterpillar

Caterpillar of a Monarch Butterfly
(actual size)

Chapter 12

Inspiration

The second stage in the life cycle of the butterfly is the larva, which we commonly call a caterpillar. The caterpillar of most species has a long, worm-like body that is thickest around the middle and tapers towards each end. The under side is flattened.

The body consists of thirteen segments, the first being the head. Each of the next three segments has a pair of "true legs" that correspond to the legs of the adult butterfly later on. There are five pairs of "prolegs" that are not really legs. Instead, they have claws or hooks for gripping as the caterpillar moves around the plant. These prolegs exist in this stage only.

> A funny fact about these critters is how they breathe. Caterpillars "breathe through tiny openings on the sides of their bodies called spiracles. (The spiracles are in their cuticle, like our skin). The holes open into a system of tubes in their body (called trachea) that carry the oxygen all over their bodies."[1]

---

1. "NatureMapping Animal Facts: Monarch Butterfly."

Stage Two | The Caterpillar

Most butterflies have about nine pairs of spiracles. According to Judy Burris, the spiracles on a butterfly "are so close to the ground, caterpillars can easily drown, even in a puddle."[2]

The ability to breathe is important for all of us. Human bodies need air to survive, and our brains need air if they are to function properly. "Permanent brain damage begins after only 4 minutes without oxygen, and death can occur as soon as 4 to 6 minutes later."[3]

One of the English words meaning "to breathe in" is inspire. Inspiration is the process of drawing air into the lungs so that the circulatory system can distribute the oxygen throughout the body. Used this way, inspiration is a synonym of inhalation.

But inspiration has an entirely different meaning as well. This other sense of inspire means to motivate or encourage. It can be an idea or a force that exerts "an animating, enlivening, or exalting influence." It refers to what takes place in the emotion, the psyche, or the spirit when a person is "influenced, moved, or guided by divine or supernatural inspiration." Inspiration provides encouragement and hope. It prods us towards action. And it gives us strength and the stamina to hang in there when circumstances look bleak.

As *Butterfly Believers*, we sometimes experience discouragement. Life gets tough, and we go through dark days. In times like these, we need the fresh inspiration of the Holy Spirit.

Several places in the Bible speak of inspiration. The first that comes to mind is in the Genesis account of creation, where it says "the Lord God formed a man from the dust of the ground and breathed into his nostrils the breath of life, and the man became a living being" (Genesis 2:7). The way he imparted life to us was through inspiration. Another scripture is in the Gospel of John where it says Jesus breathed on his disciples and said, "Receive the Holy Spirit" (John 20:22). Then in 2 Timothy 3:16, Paul writes, "All Scripture is God-breathed."

In 2017, Joe Mettle released a song titled "This Is the Air I Breathe." The opening words convey the importance of inhaling

2. Burris, 7.
3. CPR - adult and child.

Inspiration

the presence of the Lord: *This is the air I breathe, This is the air I breathe, Your holy presence, Living in me.*

Life itself. The Holy Spirit. The scriptures. All are the result of the inspiration of the Lord himself. The caterpillar takes in air through its spiracles, but a *Butterfly Believer* will inhale deeply the life-giving, spirit-sustaining oxygen that can only come from the Lord himself.

Chapter 13

Creative Genius

THE PREVIOUS CHAPTER DESCRIBED the similarities found in the majority of caterpillars, but the fact remains that there is a lot of variety. This was true in the first stage (egg), it is true here in the second stage (caterpillar), and it will be true in the third and fourth stages, too (chrysalis and imago).

Some caterpillars are short, others are long. Some are oval or slug-shaped, while others are "sometimes curiously modified by ridges and prominences."[1] Dick Vane-Wright shows a photo of the brilliantly-colored and ornate caterpillars of Morpho Telemachus, which are "as spectacular as the huge 'Morpho' butterflies they will eventually become."[2] Some caterpillars have knobs, protrusions, spikes, or humps. Others look like bird droppings or cartoon drawings. Various larvae are designed with solids, stripes, bands, and geometric shapes. Pick any color out of the largest box of crayons, and there's probably a caterpillar to match.

---

1. Holland, *The Butterfly Book*, 6.
2. Vane-Wright, *Butterflies*, 11.

Creative Genius

Why such diversity in the world of insects? I think it's because the Lord is a creative genius who loves to experiment and show off his artistic talent and palette. The same exotic creativity can be seen in fish, birds, snakes, flowers, stars, planets, and galaxies. Seven times, it says in Genesis chapter one, the Lord looked at what he had fashioned, *And God saw that it was good.*[3]

God says the same about human beings of every size, shape, ethnicity, personality, background, nationality, age, and gender. John 3:16 applies to every one of us, and nobody is excluded because the love of God is just as strong and just as rich for all of us. In Acts 10:34, Peter makes a startling observation. *I now realize how true it is that God does not show favoritism but accepts from every nation the one who fears him and does what is right.*

As I am writing this, my wife is reading a news report about another incidence of racially motivated violence. What goes through my mind are the statements in the New Testament that although it might be like that among the people "out there," that's not the way it will be among *Butterfly Believers.*

The Lord loves all people, and we love all people. The Lord shows compassion to all, and we show compassion to all, whether they are:

- white and black with yellow spots like the Queen caterpillar.
- ugly, splotched, and shriveled like the Red-spotted Purple.
- glossy orange with white markings and black spines like the Variegated Fritillary.
- bright green with symmetrically placed blue ovals and huge false eyes like the Spicebush Swallowtail.

The Lord came to serve and lay down his life for all, and we are called to serve and lay down our lives for all. As it says in 1 John 4:7–8:

> *Dear friends, let us love one another, for love comes from God. Everyone who loves has been born of God and knows*

---

3. Genesis 1:4, 10, 12, 18, 21, 25, 31.

Stage Two | The Caterpillar

God. Whoever does not love does not know God, because God is love.

CHAPTER 14

One Head or Two

IN MANY ORGANISMS, THE head is the most important part of the body. This is certainly true for the caterpillar. According to Holland, the head of a caterpillar is always conspicuous.[1] It's made of a hard, horned substance, and even though the overall size may vary from one species to another, the head is rarely small. It's almost always "large, hemispherical, conical, or bilobed."[2] The head is designed for eating, for self-defense, for seeing and sensing, and for making decisions.

Why is this fact relevant? The New Testament makes it clear that Christ is the head of the Church. This is one of the main themes in both Ephesians and Colossians. We read in Ephesians 1:22–23, *And God placed all things under his feet and appointed him to be head over everything for the church, which is his body.* Colossians 1:18 says:

> *And he is the head of the body, the church; he is the beginning and the firstborn from among the dead, so that*

---

1. Holland, *The Butterfly Book*, 6.
2. Ibid.

Stage Two | The Caterpillar

> *in everything he might have the supremacy. For God was pleased to have all his fullness dwell in him.*

Just as the head of a caterpillar is the most prominent and important part of the body, so with *Butterfly Believers* there is a recognition that Jesus Christ is our head, the most important part of our lives as individuals, and the most important part of our corporate life in the church. If we use the caterpillar as a model, Jesus's role in the church is to nourish us, defend us, provide guidance for us, and let us know what is best for us personally and for the church as a fellowship. F.F. Bruce, in his commentary on the Epistle to the Colossians, puts it this way:

> Christ and his people are viewed together as a living entity: Christ is the head, supplying life and exercising control and direction; his people are his body, individually his limbs and organs, under his control, obeying his direction, performing his work. And the life which animates the whole is his risen life, which he shares with his people.[3]

As long as we recognize Christ as our head and follow his lead, we'll be OK. But when we begin to think we can be autonomous, that it's OK to take the prominent, leading role in our own lives, and become our own head, that's when we get into trouble. The same is true for a congregation. Yes, we need human organizational leaders for practical reasons. But even so, there is a recognition that their main role is to follow Christ's headship. That's why one friend of mine refers to pastors as *undershepherds*, Christ himself being the real shepherd.[4]

Some caterpillars have a false head at the tail end, this false head usually consisting of colorations and markings that give the appearance to potential predators that this "beast" is dangerous and aggressive. In other words, it's a ruse that can be effective as

---

3. Bruce, *NICNT*, 68.
4. Keith Travis: chaplain, pastor, professor, author, undershepherd.

a defense mechanism.[5] Some of them look amazingly menacing. But the truth of the matter is that they have only one head, not two.

In our lives, whenever we establish anyone else as the head, instead of the Lord Jesus Christ, we are certainly headed for trouble. And having a false head doesn't work in the human world or the spiritual realm. So, let's establish in the earliest stages of our lives as *Butterfly Believers* that there will only be one head, and his name is Jesus.

---

5. Breyer, "8 Spectacular Caterpillars That Look Like Snakes."

Chapter 15

Built to Eat

THE RAISON D'ETRE FOR any caterpillar is to make it to the next stage, and to do that, it needs to eat. In fact, the caterpillar is designed for that very activity. It is built to eat.

With all major body parts intact from the onset, this miniature muncher is ready and able to do what it does best. Eat! With a hardened head full of mandibles or primitive teeth, six simple eyes, usually located by the mouth (where they are most needed) and eight pairs of legs (three pairs of true legs and five pairs of false or velcro type prolegs), a caterpillar is equipped with all it needs to be the "Voracious Eating Machine" that Mother Nature intended.[1]

Caterpillars are always hungry because they have to store up enough energy for the next stage of *metamorphosis*. "For a couple of weeks on average, depending on the weather, they do nothing but eat."[2] The appetite of the caterpillar is so well known, in fact, that there's a best-selling children's book titled *The Very Hungry*

---

1. D'Angelo, "The Butterfly Dimension: Caterpillar."
2. Burris, *The Life Cycles of Butterflies*, 5.

Caterpillar, and it is sold somewhere in the world approximately every thirty seconds.[3]

The first thing many caterpillars eat after emerging from the egg is the shell of the egg they've been living in. As soon as the egg is consumed, they immediately start eating the host plant their mother laid the egg on, and they'll spend the entire larval stage on that plant, if there's enough food there. Quite literally, they eat themselves out of house and home.

The average caterpillar (if there is such a thing!) eats so much that that it will gain over a thousand times it's weight before it's ready to create the chrysalis. Some estimates put the weight gain at more than three thousand times its original weight. Eating is essential for survival, health, and growth, and the same is true for *Butterfly Believers*.

> A proper diet of spiritual food is needed so Christians do not become weak and weary, but rather thrive spiritually in their relationship with God. Regular nourishment for the soul is vital for the Christian life, just as physical food is for the body.[4]

What does a *Butterfly Believer* eat? If you want to grow strong and healthy spiritually, if you want to survive the attacks of the evil one, if you want to overcome temptation, if you want to experience the joy of the Lord in your daily life, and if you want to make it to the next stage in your walk with the Lord, there are three ways to feed your spirit, and they all start with a W: the Word of God, the Will of God, and the Worship of God.

WORD OF GOD

When Jesus was being tested in the wilderness, he quoted Deuteronomy 8:3.

> The tempter came to him and said, "If you are the Son of God, tell these stones to become bread." Jesus answered,

3. Wikipedia article on *The Very Hungry Caterpillar*.
4. "What Is Our Spiritual Food?"

Stage Two | The Caterpillar

> "It is written: 'Man shall not live on bread alone, but on every word that comes from the mouth of God'" (Matthew 4:3–4).

The Bible refers to the Word of God as milk, meat, bread, and honey.[5] It's there to help us grow strong and mature in our faith, but anyone who doesn't take advantage of it is like a man who has food in the cupboard, yet he is starving to death because he won't get off the sofa, walk into the kitchen, and open the cupboard to get the food. He is like a Monarch caterpillar that lives on a milkweed plant but refuses to eat. There's food all around, but it is starving.

WILL OF GOD

According to the Gospel of John, when Jesus and his disciples arrived in Samaria, the disciples went into town to buy some food, but Jesus remained near a well, where he had a conversation with a woman who came to draw water. When the disciples returned, they urged him to eat the food they brought him. His reply confused them at the time, but can be helpful for us today, because doing what God wants us to do will feed or nourish us spiritually.

> He said to them, "I have food to eat that you know nothing about." Then his disciples said to each other, "Could someone have brought him food?" "My food," said Jesus, "is to do the will of him who sent me and to finish his work" (John 4:8, 31–32).

WORSHIP OF GOD

Focusing on the Lord Himself is another way of feeding your spirit. The combination of the music, the words we sing or speak, and the presence of the Lord serve to build us up in the inner being. There's also something about being with other believers who are also worshipping that strengthens and feeds us. In 1 Corinthians 14:1–4,

---

5. Ibid.

Built to Eat

Paul indicates that one of the reasons for corporate worship, including using our spiritual gifts, is that we might strengthen, edify, and encourage one another.

Caterpillars are indeed built to eat. They do it instinctively, right from the start, every single day. They don't forget. They don't get too busy. And they don't get distracted. May the Lord give *Butterfly Believers* that same instinct!

Chapter 16

Sensing the World

CATERPILLARS HAVE TWELVE SIMPLE eyes, six on each side of the head, but they are not able to see images or shapes.[1] All that their eyes can sense are light and dark. They do have a sense of taste. According to Ben Marcus, co-editor-in-chief of *Science Unsealed*, a caterpillar doesn't have a tongue. "Instead, its taste buds are in the mandible, and although it can taste sweet, salty, bitter, and umami,"[2] caterpillars are most sensitive to sweet versus bitter, and they like sweet best.

Another method of sensing is accomplished by small "organs of touch"[3] near the mouth. These *palpi* (plural of *palpus*) are the caterpillar's most important means of sensory perception, because lacking the ability to see, they use the *palpi* as a primitive GPS when crawling along the plant's leaf or stem. They literally feel which way to go.

1. "Butterfly Life Cycle."
2. Marcus, "Do Caterpillars Have Tongues?"
3. Holland, *The Butterfly Book*, 6.

Sensing the World

Butterfly Believers have a much more developed system of sensory perception. In addition to our five senses, we have a highly developed brain that enables us to process the information we receive.

Even more importantly, we have a spirit which differentiates us from all other life forms. It is this spiritual dimension that allows us to have a relationship with God, who is spirit. Jesus told the woman at the well, *God is spirit, and his worshipers must worship in the Spirit and in truth* (John 4:24). What he means is that we have a fantastic opportunity to "hear" the voice of the Lord, to "see" him at work in our lives and in the world, to "feel" his presence, to "touch" the hem of his garment, and to "taste" his goodness and sweetness.

In Psalm 34, we are invited to *Taste and see that the Lord is good*. We can know him intimately and experience the sweetness of his presence in our lives. But doing this requires that we patiently and gradually develop a spiritual awareness and sensitivity. *Butterfly Believers* who spend time in the Word, in Worship, and doing the Will of God often discover that they can live on a much higher level than ever imagined.

Chapter 17

No Offense

THE BODY OF A caterpillar is covered by a thin skin,[1] but it doesn't stretch, and it cannot grow. The skin starts out soft and pliable, but soon becomes rigid and hard like a shell.[2]

Have you ever heard someone referred to as being thin-skinned? To be thin-skinned is to be overly sensitive to criticism or slights. Thin-skinned people are easily offended or hurt. They take rejection, disappointment, and failure very hard. Being left out of anything might be perceived as a major insult. And they often hold a grudge. On the other hand, they are sometimes insensitive about how they come off to others. As we mature, it can be helpful to develop a little thicker skin so we can be big enough to take the inevitable slights and criticisms in stride.

When I was in high school, there was a man in the church who decided to take me under his wing. He had heard that I felt called to the ministry, and he wanted to mentor me. I was sixteen years old; he was seventy-six.

---

1. Holland, *The Butterfly Book*, 7.
2. Rosenblatt, "My Skin's Too Tight."

One Sunday after church, he came up to me and said, "Young man, if you are called to the ministry, you need to know the scriptures. Tell ya what I'm gonna do. Every Sunday when you come to church, I'm gonna give you a new Bible verse to memorize. The next week, I'll quiz you on it to make sure you know it, and then I'll give you a new verse. But every week, the quiz will gradually get longer, because I will quiz you on all the verses I've given you. OK?"

Brother Bob didn't give me an option. He made the decision, and I had no choice but to cooperate. We did this for a year-and-a-half until I graduated from high school and left for Bible college. The very first verse he selected was Psalm 119:165. He used the King James Bible, which says: *Great peace have they which love thy law: and nothing shall offend them.*

That verse has stayed with me through the years. Even though I tend to use a newer translation of the Bible now, and instead of *offend* it may be better translated as *Great peace have those who love your law, and nothing can make them stumble* (NIV), what I learned from Brother Bob and that verse in the KJV was foundational to developing a thicker skin as a *Butterfly Believer*, because regardless of what other people might do, *the peace of God, which transcends all understanding, will guard my heart and mind* (Philippians 4:7, slightly personalized). This results in an inner strength and calm so that I don't have to take offense at what people might do or say. I can be bigger and more mature.

When I look at the way Jesus was treated by his critics and opponents, I sometimes wonder how he managed to keep on loving them. Apparently, understanding his identity and his mission enabled him to rise above the circumstances he faced. He kept on loving people and stayed on target. It seems the Apostle Paul grew to that same understanding, because despite the criticism, opposition, and persecution he endured, he was able to say,

> *I have fought the good fight, I have finished the race, I have kept the faith. Now there is in store for me the crown of righteousness, which the Lord, the righteous Judge, will*

Stage Two | The Caterpillar

award to me on that day—and not only to me, but also to all who have longed for his appearing (2 Timothy 4:7–8).

Chapter 18

We're Not Clones

Some parts of a caterpillar look a lot like the corresponding parts of a butterfly. For example, a caterpillar has a head, legs, and a body. Butterflies have those body parts, too. But as we'll see in the last section of this book, they're not the same head, legs, and body. Plus, there are some brand-new features on the adult insect that aren't there in the larva—such as wings, reproductive organs, and a proboscis (tongue). We'll discuss these later, also.

The focus here is on the fact that there are some parts that remain, and others that don't. The question that immediately comes to mind is this: *When a Butterfly Believer begins to grow spiritually and experience the transformation, what remains and what doesn't?*

That's a great question, and the answer is a little tricky because in the same way that there is a lot of variety among species of butterflies, there will be many significant differences among *Butterfly Believers*. We're not expected to be identical twins, and we're not clones of the pastor, the church, or the denomination. We have different personalities, interests, and spiritual giftings. We live in different cultures, families, and political structures. We have differences in education, finances, and life experience. We may also have different rates of growth, and a different sequence of the areas in our lives that need to change.

We also understand that there is the general will of God for all of us . . . and a personal will of God that is unique to each of us. With these tremendous varieties of differences among us, we can't afford to become legalistic or dogmatic. Therefore, what follows are some generalizations and suggestions you might want to consider.

Some aspects of life that remain as you grow spiritually are your personality, personal relationships, and your career. As you grow closer to Christ, the Lord might want you to reach out in love and friendship to those you are already close to in your family, among your friends, and at work. So unless there's a reason to believe that the personal will of God for you is to make some changes, perhaps it would be better to stay where you are. What seems to be a general rule is stated several times in 1 Corinthians chapter seven.

> *Brothers and sisters, each person, as responsible to God, should remain in the situation they were in when God called them* (1 Corinthians 7:24).

On the other hand, there may be some major changes of character, moral behavior, identity, and reputation, and these should be considered prayerfully with your pastor, mentor, or small group leader. Some people change personal habits such as smoking, cussing, or drinking alcohol, especially if in the past they had a problem with any of these areas. Those who've had a history of destructive tendencies towards self, others, animals, or the planet should realize that those behaviors are inappropriate in the new lifestyle they're forming as followers of Christ. Others might want to reconsider their use of personal finances, and think about tithing, saving, paying off debt, and giving to others, while at the same time determining whether gambling or cheating on taxes are appropriate actions for *Butterfly Believers*.

We're Not Clones

A lot of people who grow closer to the Lord experience a wonderful increase in happiness and personal fulfillment, and may adopt a positive outlook on life for the very first time. Also, if you haven't found a friendly group of fellow *Butterfly Believers* to worship and grow with, I would recommend looking for a good church or fellowship.

Another complexity is trying to find a balance between personal freedom and responsibility to others, because there may be some disagreements about which behaviors are good and which should be avoided. Romans chapter fourteen is a discussion about how to handle this kind of situation. The first century Christians had differences of opinion regarding several key issues, and they got to the point of judging and criticizing one another. Many of them thought they were spiritually superior to those who disagreed with them. Paul's guidance was for them to honor and respect each other in love, even if that meant letting go of their personal freedom.

There are three statements in Romans chapter fourteen worth mentioning here.

> Verse 12: *So then, each of us will give an account of ourselves to God.*
>
> Verse 17: *The kingdom of God is not a matter of following the rules, but of righteousness, peace and joy in the Holy Spirit.*
>
> Verse 19: *Let us therefore make every effort to do what leads to peace and to mutual edification.*

These issues will become important when the caterpillar approaches the time of entering the chrysalis and emerging as a mature *Butterfly Believer*

CHAPTER 19

Ornaments

THE BODIES OF CATERPILLARS have a huge variety of decorations, or ornamentation.[1] Many of them are practically smooth, some are a bit furry or fuzzy, while others may have spikes, projections, or spines. The colors of caterpillars are also remarkable, not only in their variety and brilliance, but also in the intricate and sometimes comical designs. My favorites are those with the false heads or false eyes that are "painted" on. Some of them look like snakes, alligators, or comic strip drawings, such as the caterpillar of the Spicebush Swallowtail Butterfly.[2]

Butterfly Believers also have ornamentations that make us attractive and interesting. The first ornament is the Fruit of the Spirit.

> But the fruit of the Spirit is love, joy, peace, forbearance, kindness, goodness, faithfulness, gentleness and self-control. Against such things there is no law. Those who belong to Christ Jesus have crucified the flesh with its passions and

---

1. Holland, *The Butterfly Book*, 8.
2. Burris, *The Life Cycles of Butterflies*, 33.

Ornaments

desires. Since we live by the Spirit, let us keep in step with the Spirit (Galatians 5:22–25).

When the apostle uses the term Fruit of the Spirit, he's using the language of agriculture, and in Galatians chapter five, the Fruit of the Spirit is something that can only grow, flourish, and be sustained by the Spirit of the Lord. According to Robert Hensel, the New Testament makes it "clear that man can prepare for and encourage the growth of fruit by his labours, but he can expect and receive it only as a gift."[3]

Some might point out that these traits can be seen among many non-Christians, also. My response to that is twofold. One, it is true that there are many people in our world who exhibit the character and personality traits listed as the *Fruit of the Spirit*. I have met many non-Christians who are joyful, wonderful, loving, and kind. However, even among non-Christians, it is the Holy Spirit who graciously makes it possible for human beings to enjoy the works of his hand, the same way people of all faiths and cultures breath the air, drink the water, and eat the harvest of the Earth. It is the Lord who created it all for their benefit.

Two, it is my belief that the height of these traits cannot be fully experienced apart from a full submission to the Lordship of Jesus Christ. As the Holy Spirit fills us, leads us, speaks to us, and shapes us, we grow more fully into his likeness and increasingly exhibit his character traits.

Another ornament of *Butterfly Believers* is what I refer to as the *One-Anothers of the New Testament*.[4] Whereas the *Fruit of the Spirit* is an individual ornament, the *One-Anothers of the New Testament* are an adornment for a group of people in relationship, in this case the body of Christ. They are the characteristics and behaviors of people who interact with each other in ways that bring out the best in each other.

Consider these statements from the New Testament One-Anothers that are directed toward all Christians:

---

3. Brown, vol.1, 722.
4. See the complete list in the back of this book.

Stage Two | The Caterpillar

Wash one another's feet. Honor one another. Serve one another. Carry each other's burdens. Be humble toward one another. Consider others better than yourselves. Bear with one another. Submit to one another. Every follower of Christ is included, because that's the way we are commanded to live. . . . The world is a better place, and relationships work better.[5]

This ornament is closely related to the *Fruit of the Spirit*. In fact, we might consider the *One Anothers of the New Testament* to be an outward enactment of the internal work of the Lord called the *Fruit of the Spirit*. When the people of God cooperate with the Holy Spirit in his producing the *Fruit of the Spirit* in us, and then treat each other the way the *One-Anothers* instruct us to, the impact is far reaching, resulting in healing, restoration, encouragement, personal strength, and inner peace, and our transformation is well under way.

---

5. Linzey, *WisdomBuilt*, 134.

Chapter 20

It's a War Out There

In my opinion, anything worth doing is better if it's fun, and maybe not worth doing at all if it's not fun. This is true for life, work, church, marriage, school, hobbies, and more.

When I was an Army chaplain in an infantry battalion, there was a staff meeting where the battalion commander asked each staff officer to make one suggestion as to what we could do to improve the unit. As we went around the table, a lot of ideas were voiced and then written on a chart.

When it was my turn to speak up, I suggested that we needed to add some fun to our schedule, maybe set aside some time for the guys[1] to play basketball during the workday, and even make our training events fun. The overwhelming response by everyone in the room, including the commander, was something like, "Are you crazy, Chaplain? This is the Army. It's not supposed to be fun."

"Yes," I replied. "Protecting our nation is a serious business. But retention is down. Morale is terrible. Nobody likes coming to work. Our soldiers go home grumbling at the end of the day. If we

---

1. There were no women in an infantry battalion at the time.

Stage Two | The Caterpillar

were to add just a little bit of fun to the schedule, it would make things a lot better for everyone in the battalion, and would even make things better for our soldiers' home life."

As they scoffed and ridiculed me, a general walked in unannounced. We all jumped to our feet and stood at attention. The general went to the front of the room, told us to be seated, and said, "I'm not going to take up too much of your time, but I want to talk to you about the need to have fun in your battalion. It'll help morale and retention, and will improve overall performance, and enable you to accomplish your mission better. You've got to do something to make this unit worth being in." He spoke for about ten minutes, then left just as suddenly as he had arrived. I had never met the general, and certainly had no idea he was planning to talk about having fun that day at our staff meeting, but apparently, I wasn't the only one who understood the importance of having fun.

Individuals and societies have a variety of methods to defend and protect themselves, and so do caterpillars. Many of them are camouflaged so that they blend in with the color scheme of their host plant. Some emit a powerful odor, sort of like that of a skunk.

> The majority of caterpillars, when attacked by insect or other enemies, defend themselves by quickly hurling the anterior part of the body from side to side.[2]

Some caterpillars survive because they taste bad, and after a while, predators know about that bitter taste and leave them alone. There are others that "weave webs of silk" in a tree, the resulting "house" protecting them from the weather and their enemies.[3]

But there are some defense mechanisms that are fun to watch, like the caterpillars that actually look like bird poop. What predator wants to swoop down and eat a chunk of that? Earlier in this book, I mentioned those that have brightly colored fake eyes, making would-be attackers think the critters are bigger than they really are.

2. Holland, *The Butterfly Book*, 9.
3. Ibid., 8.

It's a War Out There

And there are quite a few unique individuals whose design allows them to protect themselves by scaring away potential predators. Like the caterpillar that resembles a snake. Or the brownish-beige caterpillar that curls its pointed tail up, and looks remarkably like a scorpion. Or the one whose tail end is painted to look like an alligator or a crocodile. It's so much fun to learn about these fascinating details.

Nevertheless, protection and defense are serious for the caterpillar, and the same is true for *Butterfly Believers*. The Apostle Paul concludes his letter to the Ephesian believers with a powerful statement about why we need to put on the Armor of God.

> *Finally, be strong in the Lord and in his mighty power. Put on the full armor of God, so that you can take your stand against the devil's schemes. For our struggle is not against flesh and blood, but against the rulers, against the authorities, against the powers of this dark world and against the spiritual forces of evil in the heavenly realms. Therefore put on the full armor of God, so that when the day of evil comes, you may be able to stand your ground, and after you have done everything, to stand. Stand firm then, with the belt of truth buckled around your waist, with the breastplate of righteousness in place, and with your feet fitted with the readiness that comes from the gospel of peace. In addition to all this, take up the shield of faith, with which you can extinguish all the flaming arrows of the evil one. Take the helmet of salvation and the sword of the Spirit, which is the word of God. And pray in the Spirit on all occasions with all kinds of prayers and requests* (Ephesians 6:10–18).

Paul understood that the devil is a schemer who will do everything possible to destroy the church. He knew that Satan is powerful, with a lot of weapons at his disposal. The apostle was also well aware of the fact that we humans are powerless in ourselves to fight a spiritual battle. So he explains what it takes to fight the good fight and win. The full Armor of God includes the following items.

The Belt of Truth
The Breastplate of Righteousness
The Shoes of Preparedness

Stage Two | The Caterpillar

The Shield of Faith
The Helmet of Salvation
The Sword of the Spirit
Praying in the Spirit

Truth. Righteousness. Preparedness. Faith. Salvation. The Word of God. Praying in the Spirit. This is what it will take for *Butterfly Believers* to fend off predators, protect themselves, survive, and make it to the next level. We can't afford to slack off and ignore the apostle's warnings, because taking the spiritual battle seriously is crucial if we want to overcome the inevitable struggles, temptations, and pitfalls.

On the other hand, investing in your relationship with Christ can be a lot of fun. I would encourage you to look for creative ways to engage in each aspect of the Armor of God. After all, morale is an important factor in retention, and the goal is to stay faithful your entire life and not give up.

When Jesus was teaching his disciples about the signs of the end times in Matthew 24:13, he made this comment: *The one who stands firm to the end will be saved.*

Therefore, let's do whatever it takes to stand firm to the end. Not just the end of the Caterpillar Stage of Existence, but all the way to the end of our lives, or until Jesus comes. It'll be worth it for all eternity.

Chapter 21

Friendship and Fellowship

Although there are a few examples of caterpillars living, working, eating, and interacting in community, most of them lead a lonely life. You might say the minority of caterpillars are extroverts, while the vast majority are introverts. Theirs is a solitary existence.

Introverts and extroverts exist among *Butterfly Believers*, too. Studies show that the percentages may be different in various people groups. There are families, nations, cultures, and careers that tend to favor one or the other. But generally speaking, it's pretty close to being a 50/50 situation, about half of us being introverts, the other half being extroverts.[1]

But there's some evidence that many of us aren't just one or the other. Carl Jung believed there was a third group, and that this third group was the most numerous.[2] One psychologist refers to this third group as "ambiverts—people with balanced, nuanced

---

1. Houston. *PositivePsychology.com*.
2. Beaton, *Psychology Today*.

Stage Two | The Caterpillar

personalities composed of both introverted and extroverted traits."[3]

This is important to keep in mind when we think about the dynamics of participating in a fellowship group or a congregation. By their very nature and definition, the terms *synagogue, congregation, assembly,* and *church* refer to a collection of people, but the people in those groups often have a variety of relationship styles and preferences. There may be introverts, extroverts, and ambiverts in the same gathering. Some people want to sit there and be left alone, some are willing to engage with others right from the start, and others want to proceed more slowly.

There's no doubt that human interaction is needed by almost every human being. We all need a friend, someone to talk to, someone who will listen to our stories and life experiences and who will share theirs with us. This is why people form associations, clubs, and activity groups. There's a need to connect with others. Sometimes this need is met by being in a stadium with 70,000 people, and sometimes being in a book group with five people is better. For this reason, Pete Wagner taught that an effective church will have a balance of large groups, medium-sized groups, and small groups. He referred to these various sizes as "celebration, congregation, and cell."[4]

Because the social dynamic is an important part of growing as a *Butterfly Believer*, I would encourage you to look for a fellowship or congregation that feels right to you, where the people are friendly and personable, yet give you room to be yourself and get involved at your own pace. If you like anonymity, then find a large congregation. If you prefer interacting on a more intimate level, look for a smaller church or one that has a variety of classes or fellowship groups.

Wherever you are, the dynamics and practices described in the *One-Anothers of the New Testament* are a great way to gauge whether it's the right place for you. The people should be affirming, honest, and kind. The preaching should encourage and inspire

3. Ibid.
4. Wagner, *Your Church Can Grow.*

Friendship and Fellowship

you. The group dynamics should be interesting and fun to participate in. The people should welcome you and invite you to various activities and events, but allow you to take your time, as well as decide for yourself what you want to do and not do.

As you continue to grow and mature, you'll probably discover that you have something to contribute to the group. You'll make friends and have opportunities to speak into people's lives. You'll be able to participate in the *One-Anothering*, helping to make it a healthy place to worship and fellowship.

Acts 2:42–47 talks about the early Christian church and some of the ways they interacted with each other. They loved each other. They helped each other when there was a need. They were loyal to one another. They spent time in each other's homes. They prayed and worshipped together. The result was a powerful move of God that transformed them and their society. My hope is that you would be part of a great friendship group like that.

Chapter 22

Personal Assessment

Caterpillars are designed to eat, and by the end of this stage, they increase somewhere between a thousand and three thousand times their weight. They grow longer and fatter every single day, but their skin doesn't grow with them.

In order for a caterpillar to grow larger than the skin it had when it hatched, it must make a new, larger skin! The caterpillar does this by first growing a new skin underneath the outer skin. Then, when it is ready, it sheds the old skin and the newer, larger skin underneath is exposed. This process is called molting.[1]

A caterpillar might molt five or six times before forming a chrysalis. Some may shed their skin twice that number of times.

Butterfly Believers are also growing. Sometimes this spiritual transformation brings rapid changes, and at other times, the growth is much slower. Whether fast or slow, most of us, somewhere along the way, might have to shed our skin to facilitate further growth. Since we're dealing with an extended metaphor, here,

---

1. "Butterfly Life Cycle: Metamorphosis."

Personal Assessment

let me explain what I mean when I say a *Butterfly Believer* might need to molt.

I grew up in a Christian family, and at age six, accepted Jesus Christ into my heart as Lord and Savior. A year later, I attended a worship service where I felt the Holy Spirit inviting me to a closer relationship with him. It was an emotional experience, and I didn't understand it very well, so I asked my sister what was happening. She explained that as we live for Jesus, from time to time we get to a point where we're ready to grow to a new level in our faith, and that's probably what was happening.

Two years later, I had a similar experience during a Sunday evening service at our church. Then when I was fourteen, it happened again when I felt a call to the ministry. Since then, I've come to realize that every five years or so, I need to reexamine myself and my spiritual life to make sure I'm where the Lord wants me to be. And with each time of reflection or self-examination, I might discover that there are changes needed in my habits, attitudes, lifestyle, or ministry involvement.

There are times the Lord might want us to change the kind of jokes we tell. The Holy Spirit might want to correct our attitudes about people of other ethnicities, nationalities, or socio-economic status. We might need to change the way we talk about others. Or we might realize that there's room for improvement in our marriage. Sometimes, we come to a new understanding about God himself, and how he wants to relate to us in a personal covenant.

Every time we have this kind of experience, there might be some attitudes or behaviors that need to be changed, updated, or corrected. This is analogous to shedding our skin, letting go of the old self in order to put on the new as we continue to become the people the Lord is calling us to be.

Paul told the *Butterfly Believers* in Ephesus to:

> *Put off your old self, which belongs to your former manner of life, . . . be renewed in the spirit of your minds, and to put on the new self, created after the likeness of God in true righteousness and holiness* (Ephesians 4:22–24).

And he told the Colossian church:

> *Whatever you do, whether in word or deed, do it all in the name of the Lord Jesus, giving thanks to God the Father through him* (Colossians 3:17).

The goal is to continue growing, each step of the way becoming more aware of who the Lord wants us to be, and how he wants us to live and think about ourselves, other people, our world, and God himself.

Chapter 23

Time Out

CATERPILLARS ARE AMAZING IN how they are able to survive around the world. Sometimes the conditions are too hot, too dry, or too cold for growth. Or there may be no food. When any of these conditions exist, a caterpillar may have to hibernate for a while, but this is especially true during winter.

At any stage, the butterfly can "sit out" the bad times by some form of hibernation or aestivation. The life processes are almost closed down, and it doesn't move, feed, or grow. "Once it has entered hibernation . . . it often needs a reliable environmental cue, such as increasing day length, to trigger a return to active life."[1]

Every *Butterfly Believer* goes through seasons of growth and nongrowth, productivity and nonproductivity. We all experience highs and lows, times of encouragement and discouragement, days we are full of faith and days we feel like giving up the faith.

In her book titled *Anonymous*, Alicia Britt Chole describes those times in our lives when we feel like we have failed. After discussing the seeming lifelessness of winter, she writes:

---

1. Vane-Write, 13.

Stage Two | The Caterpillar

> Seasonally, we too are stripped of our visible fruit. Our giftings are hidden; our abilities are underestimated. When previous successes fade, and our current efforts falter, we can easily mistake our fruitlessness for failure.[2]

Part of Chole's message is that even during the tough times, the Lord is at work in our lives. In fact, it's when life seems bleakest that God might be accomplishing the most.

> The Father's work in us does not sleep—though in spiritual winters he retracts all advertisement. And when he does so, he is purifying our faith, strengthening our character, conserving our energy, and preparing us for the future.[3]

Several years ago, I discovered a little pamphlet called *How to Spend a Day in Prayer*.[4] This brief guide taught me how to pray, and revolutionized my spiritual life. After reading it, I started taking a day, every once in a while, just to get away by myself to pray, read the word, and worship. And by memorizing the prayer outline in the pamphlet, I'm no longer nervous about praying publicly.

Jesus periodically took time to get away by himself to pray. At least once, he went to a solitary place for forty days to fast and pray. After Saul of Tarsus converted to Christ, his name changed to Paul, and he spent several years in anonymity, growing in his newfound faith and being discipled. Much later, he became a leading apostle in the Christian movement.

Because of the ebb and flow and the ups and downs of our spiritual journey, each of us should consider planning an intentional period of hibernation from time to time. This might be in the form of a weekend retreat hosted by a local church or ministry. Or it might be something you do on your own.

This is what the hibernating caterpillar is experiencing. It is still alive and healthy, but it is waiting for the day when it'll become active once again. Then it will get on with the business of eating, growing, molting, and moving towards further transformation.

2. Chole, 2.
3. Ibid.
4. Sanny, Loren C., NavPress.

Chapter 24

Are We There Yet

TAKING A LONG ROAD trip with our kids inevitably included this half-inquiry/half-complaint. Are we there yet? No matter how many activities we planned, and regardless the number of games we played and stops we made, the question was always voiced by one of our sons, two of our sons, or all three of them.

I would guess the average caterpillar, by the time it is full-grown and has completed its allotted number of skin-sheddings, is beginning to wonder the same thing. Are we there yet?

As you're reading this book, you might even be wondering by now: *Is this caterpillar part of the story ever going to end so we can move on to the next butterfly stage? Are we there yet?*

Throughout the Bible, people asked that very question over and over again.

- The People of Israel in the wilderness for forty years
- The Jews in the Babylonian captivity for seventy years
- The psalmist who asked "How long, O Lord?"

Stage Two | The Caterpillar

- Mary and Martha, who sent for Jesus to come and heal their brother
- The man at the pool of Bethesda who wondered if he would ever be the first one into the water
- The woman who had the bleeding disorder more than twelve years
- The ten lepers who came to Jesus
- Blind Bartimaeus
- The man who was born blind
- The paralytic who was lowered through the roof
- The people of Israel who were longing for the coming of the Messiah
- *Butterfly Believers* who haven't matured as quickly as they had hoped

Waiting for our hopes and dreams to finally be fulfilled has been a major theme in literature, the dramatic arts, religion, and on the personal level since the beginning of history. There seems to be a universal longing for things to be better, for the grass to be greener, for our income to be higher, and for our relationships to be more satisfying.

> *How long, Lord? Will you forget me forever?*
> *How long will you hide your face from me?*
> *How long must I wrestle with my thoughts*
> *and day after day have sorrow in my heart?*
> *How long will my enemy triumph over me?*
> *Psalm 13:1–2*

Butterfly Believers who want to grow spiritually and *become mature, attaining to the whole measure of the fullness of Christ* (Ephesians 4:12–13), will need to learn patience, because just as certainly as it is going to happen is the fact that it's going to take longer than we had hoped. But just like in every one of the above-listed situations, including the coming of the promised Messiah, *when the set time had fully come,* it happened (Galatians 4:4).

So, I have good news for you. The time finally came for every one of the people in these stories, the time is coming for *Butterfly Believers* to grow to the next level, and the time has come for this book to move into the next stage. You are now ready to take a look at what it means to be a *Butterfly Believer* as a chrysalis, which is Stage 3 of the Butterfly Life Cycle.

Are we there yet?

Yes!

STAGE THREE

The Chrysalis

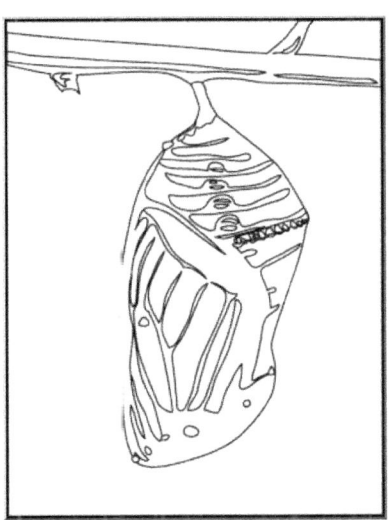

Chrysalis of a Monarch Butterfly
(approximate size)

CHAPTER 25

Foundational Attachments

When the internal clock of the caterpillar gives the signal, the fully developed, plump larva crawls over to a branch, a stone, or perhaps the eave of a house—any suitable, solid surface—and attaches itself with "a button of silk."[1] Sometimes, the caterpillar spends several hours looking for the perfect spot, and once it finds it, the most spectacular phase of its transformational journey begins: the mission of becoming what God designed it to be.

Because it needs protection from the weather and predators, being connected to something that is solid and dependable is crucial for the changes that will occur inside the chrysalis. This is also an important consideration for *Butterfly Believers* who want to grow spiritually and follow the blueprint the Lord has in mind for them.

We all need protection from the weather and predators because life isn't easy. There are pitfalls and hazards. There are forces of evil, there are false teachings, there are temptations, and there

---

1. Holland, *The Butterfly Book*, 11.

are people who will try to lead us astray. Therefore, we need to attach ourselves to something solid and dependable.

My recommendation is that you pray about a four-fold attachment. The first attachment is to the Lord himself. There is no substitute for a personal relationship with Jesus Christ. The second attachment is to the Bible, which provides the best ideological and theological foundation for our lives. Third, you need a good fellowship group where you can worship, fellowship, and receive the teaching and discipleship you need. Fourth, we all need some good Christian friends: people who are solid and dependable, who have a reputation you can trust, and who have a track record of a successful Christian lifestyle.

You have to be selective, however, because not everyone who purports to be a good Christian is worth emulating. You need to associate with people who are farther along in their metamorphic transformation than you are, people who set a godly example for how to respond to life's tough issues and situations, and who are willing to be there for you and help you walk through them.

There's a great scene in the 2002 movie version of *The Count of Monte Cristo*. Edmond Dantés was wrongly accused of treason and tossed into a dungeon prison on an island, totally discarded and removed from society. But while he was there, he met another prisoner who happened to be a Christian, a Catholic priest who mentored and discipled him. At one point, the priest said to Dantés, "As you are, I once was." The priest understood what the younger prisoner was experiencing and feeling because he had gone through exactly the same process, and had worked through the same issues and temptations. This led to a radical transformation of Edmond.

When you attach yourself to the Lord, to the Word, to a fellowship or church, and to some good Christian friends, you will have the foundation you need to enter into a spectacular phase of growing and becoming who you are designed to be.

CHAPTER 26

Appreciating Our Differences

BECAUSE CHRISTIANS AROUND THE world have the goal of growing in the grace and knowledge of our Lord and Savior Jesus Christ, there will be some characteristics that we should all have in common. The scriptures, for example teach that Christians should be honest and trustworthy. We should strive to be known for having a positive outlook on life, and for encouraging other people. We're taught to be industrious, hard-working, and dependable, yet generous to others. We're to love all people, and care about the poor and the outcast. It's been said there are two kinds of people in the world: givers and takers. Wouldn't it be awesome if Christians had a reputation for being givers?

We understand human weakness because we too are weak, but we're in the process of growing stronger and more like the Lord each day. We try to add beauty and value to our communities and to the world, to be non-judgmental people who focus on the good in others without gossiping or criticizing. We can be happy and thankful despite tough circumstances because the Lord has done so much for us.

Stage Three | The Chrysalis

Part of what makes these characteristics possible is when Christians around the world read and study the Bible, get together to worship and pray, and are involved in service projects to help others or to make a difference in our communities.

This doesn't mean we all have the same personality or that we all look alike. Nor does it imply that we agree on every point of doctrine. There are also differences in the way we conduct our worship services. In fact, we are quite different from one another, which is a good thing.

Our differences are exemplified by the variety of forms among butterfly chrysalises of different species. But what they have in common is that they provide a place for the transformation from caterpillar to butterfly by attaching themselves to something solid, then forming a protective shell.

Butterfly Believers learn to appreciate each other's differences while maintaining a sense of unity and purpose. We are called to live our lives in a way that honors the Lord and reflects his beauty, to protect others, and contribute to maintaining a setting where we all may flourish and grow personally and spiritually. It's a tall order. But then, the Lord of the butterflies is a miracle-working God who will help us accomplish the mission.

CHAPTER 27

What's on the Inside

WHEN THE APOSTLE PAUL says in Romans 12:2 *Do not conform to the pattern of this world, but be transformed by the renewing of your mind*, he's talking about the inner life. He's referring to our mind, our spirit, our attitude, our values, and our beliefs. It's this inner world that the Holy Spirit wants to make new and refashion in the image of our Creator. It encompasses what we believe and think, the way we feel about other people and ourselves, as well as our sense of right and wrong. It includes the way we talk and the decisions we make, because they inevitably influence our behavior and lifestyle.

It's important to keep in mind, however, that the godly, fully-developed inner self and identity do not reach maturity overnight. Remember, this is a lifelong process of growth and transformation. Because we were created in the Image of God and because the Holy Spirit lives inside each believer, we already have the spiritual DNA that will guide our development. Now, it's a matter of submitting to the Lord and the work he is doing in us.

Stage Three | The Chrysalis

When the caterpillar sheds its skin for the very last time and creates the chrysalis, it begins the most fantastic step of all. I'm using the word fantastic in every sense of its definition, because what happens next seems like fantasy instead of reality. It is characterized by unrestrained fancy. It is so extreme as to challenge belief. It is marked by extravagance and extreme individuality. It is excellent and superlative.[1]

As soon as the shell hardens and the caterpillar is safely inside, it turns into a thick liquid, like a soup or ooze. Then begins the mysterious process of reformulating itself, rebuilding itself, and rearranging its watery molecules into a butterfly.

The transformation of *Butterfly Believers* is also fantastic. Sometimes, the changes we experience are almost unbelievable. When the person we are on the inside is vastly different from what the Lord wants us to be, we have to be liquified and stripped down to the bare essentials before we can be rebuilt and reestablished in ways that please the Lord.

When one businessman was asked to identify the biggest change in his life when he converted to Christ, he answered, "The way I answer the telephone. I used to have to find out who was calling and then check my notes to see what I told him the last time we talked. Now, I just tell the truth all the time." One new believer stopped cheating on his wife. Another no longer gossips and bad-mouths other people. One person repented of a horrible attitude towards people of other nationalities and ethnicities. Another stopped cheating on his taxes. One convert threw away the porn. While another stopped abusing his children.

The letter to the Ephesian believers discusses some of the changes that take place when someone comes to faith in Christ.

> *You were taught, with regard to your former way of life, to put off your old self, which is being corrupted by its deceitful desires; to be made new in the attitude of your minds; and to put on the new self, created to be like God in true righteousness and holiness* (Ephesians 4:20–24).

---

1. Take a look at the definition of "fantastic" in a dictionary.

What's on the Inside

Perhaps each of us needs to take a moment to reflect on the inner self. Is what we discover pleasing to the Lord? Does it fit with how the scriptures tell us to live? The changes that take place inside the chrysalis are indeed fantastic. The changes that happen inside a *Butterfly Believer* are even more fantastic.

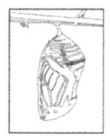

Chapter 28

Transformation

THE TRANSFORMATIONS THAT OCCUR within the confines of the chrysalis are among the most spectacular in all of nature. To go from a creeping, crawling, worm-like caterpillar to a beautiful, graceful, soaring butterfly almost defies explanation. Yet it happens, brood after brood, season after season, year after year, century after century. The same is true of *Butterfly Believers*, because Christians have been encountering the life-changing power of the Spirit of God since the beginning of human existence.

According to the Genesis account of creation, human beings were made in the image of God. But because the Fall introduced sin into the world, that image was tarnished, and human nature took a destructive path. Ever since that time, the sinful human nature has been an ugly blight to humanity, wreaking destruction in people's lives throughout the world, both on an individual and a corporate level. However, those who have had an encounter with God have been transformed and put onto a path of restoring the divine image. In essence, a life-changing encounter with the Lord is very much like being created all over again. As the apostle declared,

Transformation

Therefore, if anyone is in Christ, the new creation has come: The old has gone, the new is here! (2 Corinthians 5:17).

It's important to understand that the transformation described by the apostle is an inner change brought about by the Holy Spirit. According to W. E. Liefeld:

> In Romans 12:2 a continuing process of transformation is to characterize the believer. This is accomplished by an inner renewal of the mind and by a resistance to the influence of the world.[1]

This transformation is accompanied by a restoration of the beauty that God intended from the moment he created the world, along with a restoration of the glory of the Lord in our lives. That glory was visible on Moses's face after his encounter with God. That glory was visible when Jesus was transfigured. But the glory in us is usually seen by the changes that take place in the inner being, and are manifested by the changes in outward behavior. These changes do not necessarily mean that our circumstances in life will change. Often, the Lord saves us, restores us, and transforms us with the intent that we stay where we are and let the light of Christ shine through us in a dark place.

An example of this was when Jesus and his disciples sailed to the region of the Gerasenes, across the lake from Galilee, where he encountered a demon-possessed man. Jesus healed the man and delivered him from the power of the demons. The man wanted to go with Jesus.

> *But Jesus sent him away, saying, "Return home and tell how much God has done for you." So the man went away and told all over town how much Jesus had done for him* (Luke 8:38–39).

Paul states a general principle when he tells the Corinthian church, *Brothers and sisters, each person, as responsible to God, should remain in the situation they were in when God called them* (1 Corinthians chapter 7).

---

1. Brown, vol. 3, 864.

Stage Three | The Chrysalis

In this section of scripture, the apostle says *Butterfly Believers* should not assume that they need to change their marital status, their career field, or their place in society. Instead, it's sometimes better to remain where you are and allow the Lord to move in your life without forcing a change of situation.

The inner change that God wants to do in our lives refers to the restoration of the *Imago Dei* in us. This is the big transformation, and is usually the end product of multiple smaller transformations over time. When we allow the Lord to do his work in us, the day may come when the outward circumstances change also, but our primary concern is yielding to the inner work of the Lord. That's where his beauty and glory should be the greatest. And when that happens, watch out! You're going to be a reflection of the Lord himself.

CHAPTER 29

Magic or Miracle

BECAUSE THE BUTTERFLY "is one of nature's most perfect examples of change, transformation, and growth . . . it has long been the subject of magical folklore and legend in a variety of societies and cultures."[1] Since ancient times, people around the world have considered it to have magical or spiritual powers. These included the Greeks, Romans, Irish, Native Americans, and others.

Even nonreligious people use the term magic to describe what happens. Judy Burris, for example, says that "during the chrysalis phase, the caterpillar liquifies inside the chrysalis and reorganizes, almost magically transforming into a butterfly."[2]

Lindsay VanSomeren, who has been fascinated with butterfly metamorphosis since she was a child in a forest with her parents, explains that:

> When the larva is tucked neatly away in its cocoon or chrysalis, that's when the magic starts. Enzymes are released and literally dissolve almost the entire larva into

1. Wigington, *Learn Religions*.
2. Burris, *The Life Cycles of Butterflies*, 9.

Stage Three | The Chrysalis

a nutrient soup . . . Only a few other things remain: the nervous system, the breathing tubes, and the imaginal disks.[3]

Now the butterfly begins to rebuild itself.

Dick Vane-Wright acknowledges that "some people have viewed insect metamorphosis, from creeping caterpillar to soaring butterfly, as mysterious or even miraculous."[4] Others simply say "it happens" with no attempt at explaining the process.

The transformations in the egg and in the chrysalis are indeed fantastic and radical. The creatures that emerge are completely different from how they started out, and the process is almost impossible to explain. We know it is guided by the DNA that is present from the day the egg is fertilized, and that the molecular building blocks are present all along the way. Other than that, each transformation is amazingly remarkable and complex. Perhaps one day the process will be explained scientifically. But maybe it truly is an evidence of the miraculous hand of God at work.

I do know that the changes that occur inside human beings who become *Butterfly Believers* are often just as remarkable, just as amazing, and just as magical as the metamorphosis of the butterfly. The internal work of the Holy Spirit is invisible, but it is happening at all times. Romans 8:28 says, *We know that God is working nonstop for the good of those who love him* (paraphrased). And the apostle wrote to the Corinthian believers:

> *Therefore we do not lose heart. Though outwardly we are wasting away, yet inwardly we are being renewed day by day. For our light and momentary troubles are achieving for us an eternal glory that far outweighs them all. So we fix our eyes not on what is seen, but on what is unseen, since what is seen is temporary, but what is unseen is eternal* (2 Corinthians 4:16–18).

The work of the Holy Spirit in you is magical, it is miraculous, it is remarkable, and it is certain. So don't lose heart, thinking that

---

3. VanSomeren, *Untamed Science*.
4. Vane-Wright, *Butterflies*, 14.

God has forgotten you or that you're never going to grow strong in your faith. God isn't finished with you yet. In fact, God has plans for you. As Jeremiah 29:11 reminds us:

> *"I know the plans I have for you," declares the Lord, "plans to prosper you and not to harm you, plans to give you hope and a future."*

The Lord's plan for you will result in beauty, glory, freedom, and joy. I am confident of this because *he who began a good work in you will carry it on to completion* (Philippians 1:6), and because what shows up next in metamorphosis is the beautiful adult butterfly that is able to spread its wings and fly.

STAGE FOUR

The Imago

Monarch Butterfly
(actual size)

Chapter 30

Going Through the Fire

WHEN THE CATERPILLAR INSIDE the pupa (chrysalis) is almost finished with the remarkable transformation into a butterfly, the walls of the chrysalis become thin and transparent. You can actually see the butterfly trapped inside. But then . . . as if on cue . . . when the butterfly is ready to emerge, the chrysalis wall splits open and the head, legs, and antennae come out, followed by the wings and the abdomen. "At first, the little butterfly is rather a sorry-looking affair, crumpled and damp, the soon-to-be beautiful wings hanging like limp bags at each side."[1]

Breaking out of the shell is never an easy task. In fact, it's quite a strenuous ordeal, requiring the butterfly to push, flex, and struggle, forcing its wings against the inner walls of its cage. Some observers feel sorry for the poor butterfly and are tempted to provide assistance and help it get out. But that isn't a good idea because the butterfly needs to develop strength, making the process of breaking free an absolutely necessary step towards the ultimate goal of surviving and thriving as a mature butterfly.

1. Vane-Wright, *Butterflies*, 16.

The growth and development of *Butterfly Believers* also require that we struggle, endure hardships, and encounter difficulties that we must overcome. President Teddy Roosevelt made this observation: "Nothing in the world is worth having or worth doing unless it means effort, pain, difficulty."[2] In the New Testament, James 1:2–4 says it this way:

> *Consider it pure joy, my brothers and sisters, whenever you face trials of many kinds, because you know that the testing of your faith produces perseverance. Let perseverance finish its work so that you may be mature and complete, not lacking anything.*

According to James, the trials, tests, and tribulations are worth rejoicing about because of what they accomplish in our lives. In the same way the butterfly must work at getting out of the chrysalis, *Butterfly Believers* must experience hardship in order to develop spiritual stamina, resilience, and a faith that not only withstands the storms of life, but can also move mountains.

A few years ago, we were visiting some people who were having a tough time. It seemed like everything was going wrong in their lives, and they wondered why God didn't answer their prayers and make it all better. We told them we understood, and tried to encourage them. Suddenly, one of them said, "There's no way you can understand. You've never had a problem. Everything is always perfect in your life."

My wife and I looked at each other and almost burst out laughing. It's true that we don't talk much about the pain or the struggles we've gone through, but we've certainly had our share of pain, hardship, and life-threatening illness, including cancer. We know what it's like to wonder how we're ever going to pay the bills. We've experienced childbirth, war, and death of family members. There are people close to us who made decisions that broke our hearts. We have tasted disillusionment and failure, and have had to let go of a few dreams and hopes. We've come through a lot of temptations, tests, and trials. We understand how difficult

---

2. *Quotefancy.*

Going Through the Fire

marriage can be. We know from personal experience that life isn't easy.

We also understand that nobody becomes a mature, victorious Christian without going through the fire. But as Shadrach, Meshach, and Abednego discovered, they came out OK because the Fourth Man in the Fire was there with them.[3]

---

3. Daniel chapter 3.

Chapter 31

Restoring the Beauty

As the wings of the adult insect are filled with fluid, they expand to their full size and beauty. This is what we've been waiting for since the moment the egg was placed on the host plant a generation ago, and we are not disappointed, because butterflies come in every color imaginable, and are intricate in detail. Thousands of scales cover the wings, giving each butterfly its unique design. "Some scales are colored by pigments; others are iridescent, appearing shiny or metallic because of the way the light hits them. A few are transparent."[1]

You might want to take a few minutes right here to pause, go to your phone or computer, and look up images of butterflies just to take a fresh look at them. Better yet, you could locate a butterfly house in your area and take a look at them in person. It's easy to see why people around the world and throughout history have fallen in love with them. The brother/sister team of Judy Burris and Wayne Richards start their book with this paragraph:

---

1. Burris, *The Life Cycles of Butterflies*, 14.

Restoring the Beauty

> There's something very special about butterflies. Maybe it's their gentle nature, striking colors, or graceful flight. Butterflies have symbolic meaning in many cultures, and they've inspired artists and poets over the centuries. They've been written into fairy tales, woven into tapestries, and painted on pottery. Butterflies touch the hearts of young and old alike. And if one actually lands on you, somehow you feel honored, as if you were singled out as an especially trustworthy companion.[2]

As special and as gorgeous as butterflies are, they don't even begin to compare to the beauty that the Lord brings into the lives of his people. Anyone who has been on this planet for a while knows about pain and ugliness. We see it in others and in ourselves. It seems that the *Second Law of Thermodynamics* is true not only in the physical universe, but in our lives as well. Things in motion lose momentum. Things that are hot cool down. Things that are organized become disorganized. And, things that are pretty lose their beauty.

The same can be said of our spirituality, too. We start our journey of faith full of high hopes and good intentions. Then, things go wrong, and we become disillusioned. We lose our momentum, begin to grow cold spiritually, and things get ugly.

But Jesus comes into our lives to restore the beauty and the joy. In Luke chapter four we read about the time the Lord went into a synagogue and read from the Prophet Isaiah.

> *He went to Nazareth, where he had been brought up, and on the Sabbath day he went into the synagogue, as was his custom. He stood up to read, and the scroll of the prophet Isaiah was handed to him. Unrolling it, he found the place where it is written: "The Spirit of the Lord is on me, because he has anointed me to proclaim good news to the poor. He has sent me to proclaim freedom for the prisoners and recovery of sight for the blind, to set the oppressed free, to proclaim the year of the Lord's favor." Then he rolled up the scroll, gave it back to the attendant and sat down. The eyes of everyone in the synagogue were fastened on him.*

---

2. Ibid., 1.

Stage Four | The Imago

> He began by saying to them, "Today this scripture is fulfilled in your hearing" (Luke 4: 16–21).

To understand all that he's saying, it may be helpful to look at Isaiah chapter sixty-one, because this is the passage Jesus read to the people that Saturday morning in Nazareth. Luke's gospel recorded the first two verses of Isaiah sixty-one, but the passage goes further, and I think Jesus also fulfills the next verse in our lives, too.

> *To comfort all who mourn, and provide for those who grieve in Zion—to bestow on them a crown of beauty instead of ashes, the oil of joy instead of mourning, and a garment of praise instead of a spirit of despair. They will be called oaks of righteousness, a planting of the Lord for the display of his splendor* (Isaiah 61:3).

I really like the picture Isaiah paints for us. In his day, people who were grieving, repenting, or humbling themselves literally put ashes on their heads. However, when the Messiah or the Anointed One comes, he will bring the good news that the sorrow is over, broken hearts are mended, sins are forgiven, and hurts are healed. In addition, those who are weak will become as strong as fully established oak trees. John Oswalt explains it like this:

> The picture of the mourner, with *ashes* on the head, wrapped in sackcloth, with a *spirit* crushed by despair, is replaced by the picture of a party goer with a *beautiful headdress*, smelling of costly *oil*, and wearing a *garment of praise*.[3]

This is what Jesus claimed to be fulfilling that day. He came to bring beauty back into the lives of his people, and he continues doing that to this day. I fully expect the Lord to restore his beauty and glory in the lives of every *Butterfly Believer* who remains faithful to him. You may need to flap your wings a while to get the juices flowing. Then, allow the Holy Spirit to fill you with his love, joy, peace, and beauty.

---

3. Oswalt, *The Book of Isaiah*, 567.

Chapter 32

Design and Destiny

After emerging from the captivity of the chrysalis, the new butterfly finds a place to exercise its wings. This action pumps a blood-like fluid into the veins of the wings, causing them to expand to full size. The result is a set of wings that are sturdy and capable of sustaining flight. As soon as the wings are dry, the mature insect can fly.

There are at least seven purposes of flight: finding food, avoiding predators, locating a mate, getting to the right plant to lay eggs, finding warmth, pursuing rivals, and migrating. However, if a butterfly doesn't get enough fluid in its wings within an hour, its wings may harden before it's capable of flying, which means it will die. It won't be able to do any of the seven activities, and it won't live up to the reason it was created.

Butterfly Believers also run the risk of not living up to their calling. According to Jesus's explanation of the *Parable of the Sower* in Matthew 13:18–23, there is the danger of misunderstanding the message about the Kingdom of God. Some are at risk because they have no roots. Others have their faith choked out because of the worries and distractions of life in this world.

In 1 Corinthians 9:19–27, the Apostle Paul adds another potential problem that can disqualify us from living up to our calling. In this scripture, part of the purpose of a mature believer is to be productive in ministry while running the race effectively. Though we have considerable freedom to live how we want, it is important that we discipline ourselves. Otherwise, not only might we fail to be effective in ministry, but we are at risk of running the race in vain and missing out on the prize.

Butterflies are designed to fly, to soar, to sail high and far. Some are among the fastest flying insects; others are quite slow. Some live their entire lives in one locale, while others migrate thousands of miles. Some are graceful and smooth in their flight, but some appear to be clumsy, making you wonder how they even fly at all.

Similarly, *Butterfly Believers* have the ability to fly, soar, and sail. We are called to live our lives pleasing to the Lord according to the scriptures, running the race in such a way as not to be disqualified. I would encourage you to read the *Parable of the Sower* and Paul's description of what it takes to run the race effectively so that you will not be the one who misunderstands the message of the Kingdom of God, so you will not be choked out, plucked up, shriveled, or disqualified.

Healthy, mature *Butterfly Believers* are able to fly. They have an ability to thrive and survive. They take advantage of opportunities to gain spiritual nourishment, as well as find ways to minister to others. Plus, they increasingly manifest the beauty and glory of the Image of God. That is their design and their destiny.

Chapter 33

Disciple and Discipler

THE MISSION OF ADULT butterflies is to reproduce,[1] and they have just a short amount of time for this to happen. Within an hour after emerging from the chrysalis, mature males are capable of mating. Females are ready to mate as soon as they're out of the chrysalis, which is followed almost immediately by laying the eggs. Having completed the mission, the females will often die within a day or so, depending on the species, and males may live a few more weeks. The life cycle is now complete, and the next generation begins.

The mission of *Butterfly Believers* corresponds to that of the adult butterfly because just before Jesus ascended into heaven, he gave his disciples *the Great Commission*.

> Then Jesus came to them and said, "All authority in heaven and on earth has been given to me. Therefore go and make disciples of all nations, baptizing them in the name of the Father and of the Son and of the Holy Spirit, and teaching them to obey everything I have commanded you. And

1. Culin, "Lepidopteran"

Stage Four | The Imago

surely I am with you always, to the very end of the age" (Matthew 28:18–20).

The command to "go and make disciples" has two meanings. First, it can refer to the ministry of evangelism, leading people to faith in Christ. Second, it can refer to discipleship or spiritually mentoring other Christians. Since *the Great Commission* applies to all believers, it means we are all called to share our faith with others or help them in their own spiritual journey. In a sense, *every disciple is a discipler.*

Rick Warren's discipleship model is a baseball diamond, each base calling for a different level of commitment from each follower of Christ as he or she grows.

First Base: Commitment to Membership
Second Base: Commitment to Maturity
Third Base: Commitment to Ministry
Home Plate: Commitment to Mission

In Warren's image of the baseball diamond, the path between the bases contains a goal for each level of commitment. The goal on the way to first base is "Knowing Christ." On the way to second base, the goal is "Growing in Christ." Between second and third, the goal is "Serving Christ." And on the way to home plate, disciples are taught that "Sharing Christ" is the goal.[2] This is thoroughly in keeping with *the Great Commission.*

If an adult butterfly doesn't reproduce, it means something went wrong in its development. Similarly, *Butterfly Believers* who are growing in Christ usually find a way to participate in one aspect of the Great Commission or the other.

---

2. Warren, *The Purpose Driven Church.*

CHAPTER 34

Pollinators

EARLIER IN THIS BOOK, Chapter 15 focused on the caterpillar that was *Built to Eat*, because eating was the sole purpose in that stage of existence. All it had to do was eat and grow, and it ate the leaves and stems of its host plant because bulking up was the goal.

A mature butterfly, however, has a different anatomy and a different purpose. Yet, it still needs nourishment. Instead of eating the leaves and stems, adult butterflies eat or drink the pollen and nectar from flowering plants.

Nectar is a sugary liquid containing trace nutrients. Pollen is rich in proteins, fats, vitamins and minerals. The nutritional content of nectar and pollen varies by plant species, much like carrots and blueberries have different nutrients. Each pollinator's dietary needs depend on its species, life stage (immature or adult) and sex (female or male).[1]

The purpose of butterflies is to reproduce, and they need this more complex nutrient source so the eggs will have what they need for a healthy start to their existence. But there's another reason

---

1. Holt, "Nectar and pollen fuel pollinator life."

adults need the new diet. Whereas caterpillars merely crawled, flying butterflies require a lot more fuel and energy, much like a jet has different fuel and energy needs than a motorcycle.

As *Butterfly Believers* mature and grow, we too may need to adjust our diet from time to time. We'll always need to feed on the Word of God, the Will of God, and the Worship of God. But as we develop spiritually, we need to start *Digging Deeper*,[2] which will help us understand the Lord and the Bible better. We'll grow in our awareness of other people and their needs. We'll become healthier and stronger personally. We will develop theologically and morally. And we'll be better able to serve in ministry as opportunities arise. Peter mentions the concept of babies needing milk when he writes:

> *Therefore, rid yourselves of all malice and all deceit, hypocrisy, envy, and slander of every kind. Like newborn babies, crave pure spiritual milk, so that by it you may grow up in your salvation, now that you have tasted that the Lord is good* (1 Peter 2:1–3).

Babies are not yet ready for solid food, so in order to grow they need milk. But as they age, the day comes when they are ready for solid food. The writer of the New Testament Book of Hebrews indicates the natural progression among *Butterfly Believers* is that as they mature spiritually, they should change their diet in order to grow strong, as well as to be better prepared to serve in ministry.

> *We have much to say about this, but it is hard to make it clear to you because you no longer try to understand. In fact, though by this time you ought to be teachers, you need someone to teach you the elementary truths of God's word all over again. You need milk, not solid food! Anyone who lives on milk, being still an infant, is not acquainted with the teaching about righteousness. But solid food is for the mature, who by constant use have trained themselves to distinguish good from evil* (Hebrews 5:11–14).

---

2. *Digging Deeper* is a new devotional Bible study by Linda S. Linzey.

Pollinators

Again, notice that there is a theological and a moral dimension to our spiritual development. We know more and grow more. We understand the Bible more and understand life more. And in the process, we increasingly are being transformed into the people the Lord wants us to be. As Paul wrote to the Corinthian believers:

> *When I was a child, I talked like a child, I thought like a child, I reasoned like a child. When I became an adult, I put the ways of childhood behind me* (1 Corinthians 13:11).

There's a beautiful side effect of butterflies feeding on nectar and pollen. Because they can fly and go from plant to plant, they become *pollinators*. As they are going about their normal business as usual, they are benefitting the plants and the world around them.

I have seen this among mature Christians, too. Because of their maturity, their joie de vivre, and their interaction with people in their community, they are loved and respected wherever they go. They have become the salt of the earth and the light of the world. They are making a difference, not only by their intentional acts of service and ministry, but also by the unintentional side effects of being the *Butterfly Believers* God has called them to be.

Chapter 35

More Than Meets the Eye

When we see a butterfly on a plant or bush, we often focus on the beauty of its wings because . . . well . . . that's what grabs our attention. The colors, the patterns, the lacework, and the symmetry captivate and inspire us.

But there's so much more to a butterfly than its wings. Like all insects, butterflies have a head, a thorax, and an abdomen. The head has the eyes, the antennae, the proboscis, and the mouth. The thorax, or middle section, contains the wings and the legs, which is why some have called it the butterfly's center of locomotion.[1] The abdomen is where the heart, reproductive organs, breathing pores, and most of the digestive system are found.

All three sections of the body are vital, so it's hardly necessary to say that the wings couldn't exist without the rest of the body. Yet, external appearances are typically what we focus on. Sometimes, that's all we see.

When we look at people, we tend to do the same thing. We focus on appearances, which is why pretty people are often popular.

---

1. Vane-Wright, *Butterflies*, 53.

More Than Meets the Eye

We are overly swayed by first impressions, which can be entirely superficial. Secondarily, we are impressed by talent. People who can sing, dance, act, tell a joke, or shoot a basketball are popular and can make a lot of money. If people are attractive and talented, now that's a guaranteed recipe for stardom, even if they are lacking in intelligence or a developed sense of morality. Because of their outward appearance or their talent, we are willing to overlook the more substantial aspects of what it means to be a human being, a person, or a child of God.

We Christians do the same thing. We choose leaders who are good-looking and who can talk well in public. We admire those who play the piano or who have beautiful voices. We cater to the rich. And we avoid those who are less attractive, less talented, and less wealthy.

Since the theme of this book is *transformation*, perhaps it's time we borrowed an expression from *The Transformers*. The theme song of the original animated television show started with the lyrics, "Transformers, more than meets the eyes."

Butterfly Believers understand that there is an inner beauty that is considerably more valuable than outward appearances. Character matters more than talent. And attitude is more meaningful than how much money a person makes.

Jesus talks a lot about values and priorities in the Sermon on the Mount. For example, in Matthew chapter six, he mentions treasures, money, clothes, what we eat, who we try to please, and what we worry about. His summary is quite blunt: these are the values of the pagans.[2] Instead, the secret to living a meaningful life filled with happiness is to *seek first his kingdom and his righteousness, and all these things will be given to you as well* (Matthew 6:33).

As *Butterfly Believers* who are growing towards maturity, it's a good idea to develop the whole person, rather than merely focusing on the superficial aspects of who we are. Taking this approach, we will have so much more to offer to the people in our lives, our church, and our community.

---

2. Matthew 6:32.

CHAPTER 36

X-Ray Vision

THE FIRST FICTIONAL CHARACTER to have x-ray vision was *Olga Mesmer, The Girl with the X-Ray Eyes*, in 1937. Then came *Superman* (1938, though x-ray vision wasn't mentioned until the following year), *Ultra Boy* (1962), and *Superboy* (1993).[1] In reality, however, the only people with x-ray vision are radiologists and radiographers. Because of their training and the equipment they have access to, these specialists are able to look inside a body.

If you were to look inside the body of a butterfly, you would see the muscular system, digestive system, and nervous system. You'd notice the breathing tubes, the heart, the stomach, and the brain. You'd also find the salivary glands, silk glands, guts, reproductive organs, and, of course, much more.

But what I really wonder is what we might see if we were able to look inside a *Butterfly Believer* with spiritual x-ray vision. Would we discover a *soothing tongue* that *is a tree of life*? Or *a perverse tongue* that *crushes the spirit* (Proverb 15:4)? When peering into the brain, might we be looking at *a mind governed by the flesh*?

---

1. There are two website articles titled "X-ray Vision."

X-Ray Vision

Or possibly *a mind governed by the Spirit* (Romans 8:6)? Would we see *a pure heart* (Psalm 51:10)? Or *a heart that is deceitful above all things and beyond cure* (Jeremiah 17:9)?

Regardless of what people might look like on the outside, the heart condition is the key, and we might need to make Eddie Espinosa's song the prayer of our own heart. I have sung it and prayed it many times.

> *Change my heart Oh God, make it ever true*
> *Change my heart Oh God, may I be like You*
> *You are the potter, I am the clay*
> *Mold me and make me, this is what I pray*
> *Change my heart Oh God, make it ever true*
> *Change my heart Oh God, may I be like You*[2]

---

2. Eddie Espinosa, composer and copyright holder.

Chapter 37

Malformations

As butterflies develop, there are some curious malformations that occur.[1] Most often, the aberrations appear as added or missing colors or designs on the wings. Among some species, it's not uncommon for females to be albinos, either completely white or light-colored. And among males, there's a tendency towards melanism, which causes them to be darker or even completely black. Sometimes, a butterfly will have wings of a male attached to a female body, or a female wing on one side and a male wing on the other. This seems to be accompanied by an inability to reproduce. Another malformation is that sometimes a butterfly will show up much smaller than usual.

These aberrations have a variety of possible causes. Abnormal temperatures during the chrysalis phase can affect the developing butterfly. Some traits may be the result of genetic mutations. And there may be a variety of environmental factors involved.

Malformations also occur among *Butterfly Believers*. Paul's letters to the Corinthian church indicate that they had several

---

1. Holland, *The Butterfly Book*, 24.

Malformations

abnormalities in the congregation. There was an acceptance and a boasting about sexual immorality. They were divided into factions and were fighting and quarreling. Some of them were still involved with pagan idolatry. There were gross misunderstandings about appropriate behavior during worship services. And some serious false teachings had worked their way into the church.

Paul writes in 2 Corinthians 12:20 that the abnormalities in Corinth included *discord, jealousy, fits of rage, selfish ambition, slander, gossip, arrogance and disorder*. And in Romans 1:29–32, he mentions *greed and depravity, envy, murder, strife, deceit and malice, and people who are gossips, slanderers, God-haters, insolent, arrogant and boastful*.

In Galatians, the same apostle contrasts the desires of the flesh with the desires of the Spirit. I think it is fair to say that the behaviors listed as *Acts of the Flesh* are considered by the apostle to be abnormalities and malformations among *Butterfly Believers*. Here's what he says in Galatians 5:16–23.

> *So I say, walk by the Spirit, and you will not gratify the desires of the flesh. For the flesh desires what is contrary to the Spirit, and the Spirit what is contrary to the flesh. They are in conflict with each other.*
>
> *The acts of the flesh are obvious: sexual immorality, impurity and debauchery; idolatry and witchcraft; hatred, discord, jealousy, fits of rage, selfish ambition, dissensions, factions and envy; drunkenness, orgies, and the like. I warn you, as I did before, that those who live like this will not inherit the kingdom of God.*
>
> *But the fruit of the Spirit is love, joy, peace, forbearance, kindness, goodness, faithfulness, gentleness and self-control.*

Then, as if to punctuate his teaching about some of the abnormalities within Christianity, he says that:

> *Those who belong to Christ Jesus have crucified the flesh with its passions and desires. Since we live by the Spirit, let us keep in step with the Spirit* (Galatians 5:24–25).

Stage Four | The Imago

Normal, healthy Christianity is beautiful. It attracts people who are searching for truth and meaning in their lives. But *Butterfly Believers* who allow malformations, aberrations, and abnormalities to remain in the congregation or in their individual lives run the risk of turning people away from Christ, or of driving them away from the Church. There's also the possibility that they, too, might be in danger of dropping out of the race.

Chapter 38

Natural Interests

ONE OF MY FAVORITE features of butterflies is the wing coloration that allows them to blend in like camouflage, appear to be invisible, or look like they are actually a different creature. Three of my favorite types are Leaf Butterflies, Glasswing Butterflies, and Owl Butterflies. Let me explain.

A Leaf Butterfly has wings that are shaped, sized, and colored exactly like the leaves of nearby trees. When it lands on a branch or twig, it's almost impossible to discern that there's a vulnerable insect nearby because it looks like a leaf. Most birds who are looking for their next meal aren't interested in tasting a leaf.

A Glasswing Butterfly, on the other hand, is mostly transparent. You can literally see right through it. This form of camouflage works almost anywhere because the butterfly is practically invisible. A predator might be staring right at it, but all it can see is the plant the butterfly is resting on. Amazing!

The wings of an Owl Butterfly are brown and textured, with a large circle on each wing that looks like an eye. When the wings are folded flat, you'd think you are looking right into the face of an owl. And since owls themselves are predators, no insect-eating bird is about to attack what seems to be an owl looking straight at it. In all three examples, the natural design of the butterfly enables it to survive, thrive, and carry out its mission.

By now, you might be thinking, "OK, what possible devotional application can come from butterfly mimicry?" Here's a suggestion. Why not use your natural interests and proclivities to build relationship and rapport with the people around you, for the purpose of sharing Christ with them?

The use of common interests and hobbies has been called friendship evangelism or lifestyle evangelism, and it can be pretty effective. A church in the Atlanta area built its outreach ministry on the concept of interest-based small groups. They have discipleship groups for people interested in paintball, quilting, motorcycling, and cooking. Other groups are for young parents, sports fans, and skateboarders. I know Christians who host an annual Superbowl party, giving them an opportunity to build friendships with people who like football as much as they do.

The apostle Paul made the comment that he was determined to be *all things to all people so that by all possible means I might save some* (1 Corinthians 9:22–23). And then a couple chapters later he wrote, *Follow my example, as I follow the example of Christ* (1 Corinthians 11:1).

By using your natural interests and abilities to build relationships, you also build a reputation as someone who is dependable, trustworthy, and likeable. Eventually, the day comes when someone will ask you about your faith in the Lord, or why you are a Christian. It might be a year or two, or ten years down the road, but if you're faithful, it'll happen.

Are you a musician? A photographer? Or a geocacher? Do you like discussing the books you read or movies you see? Whatever you like to do, and whatever you are interested in, chances are there are other people in your area with similar interests and likes. Why not consider taking advantage of what's already in place to make a difference on behalf of the Kingdom of God?

Natural Interests

Just like with butterflies, the natural design of *Butterfly Believers* enables them to survive, thrive, and carry out their mission.

Chapter 39

Living Up to Our Potential

When the butterfly reaches the last stage, it's growth is complete. Having survived this far, it is now a mature insect, full of grace, charm, and beauty. It can fly, be productive, and live up to its potential in every way.

This is the goal of the *Butterfly Believer*. Christians who remain faithful, live a life of godliness, and continue to pursue the Word of God, the Will of God, and the Worship of God, gradually reach maturity in their spiritual lives. As it says in Ephesians:

> *Then we will no longer be infants, tossed back and forth by the waves, and blown here and there by every wind of teaching and by the cunning and craftiness of people in their deceitful scheming. Instead, speaking the truth in love, we will grow to become in every respect the mature body of him who is the head, that is, Christ. From him the whole body, joined and held together by every supporting ligament, grows and builds itself up in love, as each part does its work* (Ephesians 4:14–16).

Living Up to Our Potential

As mature Christians, we're no longer giving in to the same old temptations. We've overcome many of the weaknesses and habits that plagued us in the early days of following the Lord. And we don't have to struggle with every false teaching that comes along, because we're able to discern truth much better than we used to. By now, we've developed a sensitivity to the Holy Spirit, how he speaks to us, and how he leads us.

There's an important concept in the Bible that is too often misunderstood. The Hebrew word nephesh is the Old Testament word for soul. Genesis 2:7 tells us that the Lord God formed a man from the dust of the ground and breathed into his nostrils the breath of life, and the man became a living being. In other words, a human being doesn't have a soul, a human being is a soul, and the soul should be thought of as the entirety of our being. We see this in Psalm 103:1.

> *Bless the Lord, O my soul;*
> *and all that is within me, bless his holy name!*

Classic Hebrew poetry contains a feature called parallelism, in which the writer has the exact same meaning in two successive lines but uses different words, phrases, or imagery. According to the Jewish Encyclopedia:

> It is now generally conceded that parallelism is the fundamental law, not only of the poetical, but even of the rhetorical and therefore of higher style in general in the Old Testament.... The same idea is expressed in its full import ... not in a continuous, uninterrupted sentence, but in several corresponding clauses or members with different words.[1]

Therefore, in Psalm 103, "my soul" in the first line has the same meaning as "all that is within me" in the second line. That's because the soul is the being, is the breath, is the life of the person. Many Christian thinkers have taught that a human is a three-part being. If that's the case, then perhaps we should say it this way. A

---

1. Casanowicz, *Jewish Encyclopedia*.

human being is a soul, and the soul consists of the body, mind, and spirit.

What I'm leading up to is this: a mature believer understands the importance of caring for the entirety of the self. As stewards of the life God has given us, we care for the body, we develop the mind, and we practice the spiritual disciplines. This helps us mature in all aspects of our being—to the glory of God, and to the benefit of those around us.

CHAPTER 40

Butterfly Believers

*God created man and woman in his own image.
And God blessed them.*

GENESIS 1:27

AN ADULT INSECT IS officially called an imago, which means image or picture. This is the stage the butterfly looks its best, is fully developed, and fulfills its purpose. This is the stage that has captured the imagination of people around the world since the beginning of history. And this is where our discussion of the butterfly life cycle comes to a crescendo.

The butterfly is a wonderful analogy of the spiritual growth among Christians because metamorphosis means transformation, and the gradual changes from one stage to the next are so appropriate for a discussion of the changes that take place in our lives.

The fact that the adult or mature butterfly is called an imago is a fantastic part of the story. This is a powerful reminder that

Stage Four | The Imago

every *Butterfly Believer* was fashioned in the Image of God. Theologians refer to this by using the Latin phrase, *Imago Dei*.

This comes up in the Bible in some rather interesting ways. Some men tried to set a trap for Jesus one day by asking him a trick question. Is it right to pay taxes to Caesar? They expected a simple yes/no, either/or answer that would force him into a corner and get him into trouble with either the Roman authorities or the Jewish leaders. It would be a win/win for them and a lose/lose for him. But as he often did, Jesus had an interesting reply.

> *"Show Me the coin used for the tax." So they brought Him a denarius. "Whose image and inscription is this?" He asked them. "Caesar's," they said to Him. Then He said to them, "Therefore give back to Caesar the things that are Caesar's, and to God the things that are God's"* (Matthew 22:19–22).

In answering their question, Jesus avoided the obvious either/or, and totally reframed the dilemma. In the eternal scheme of things, it doesn't matter who you pay taxes to. The real issue is whose likeness is on the coin and whose picture is on you as a person, because the image shows the identity of the owner. Since Caesar's picture is on the denarius, go ahead and return it to him. It belongs to him. Likewise, because God's image is on you, he claims ownership of your life, so give back to the Lord what is rightfully his. You belong to him.

Jesus's reply turned the tables on them because they were the spiritual leaders who were supposed to understand the scriptures. They were the ones who claimed to have the image of God. Yet in reality, they were far from God.

> *Give back to Caesar what already belongs to him,*
> *and give back to the Lord what already belongs to him.*

His image, his likeness, his stamp of ownership is indelibly printed on our soul, our very being, and we have chosen to give ourselves back to him. This is what we were created for. This is our reason for being. This is what empowers us to reach our highest level of existence. This is what we were designed for.

Butterfly Believers

No matter who you are, where you are from, whether you are male or female, or what you look like, you are made in the Image of God and there's nobody in the world more important or more valuable than you. You are free to be yourself, free to pursue your dreams, free to express yourself, and free to fly. And in that freedom, you can liberate others to do the same. You are a *Butterfly Believer*. And you are beautiful.

How to Lead a Discussion Group or Class

BEFORE THE SESSION

1. Take time to pray every day for your class or discussion sessions, as well as for the individuals in the group.

2. Depending on your location and other factors, you might want to plan for refreshments, send an email reminder of when and where the meeting is happening, and mention the chapter or topics to be covered. The more you delegate these responsibilities, the more buy-in you'll get from the group.

3. Read the material in advance. Then, determine which questions, topics, and scriptures you want to handle during the session. Research the information you might want to be able to provide during the discussion. By anticipating how the class time might unfold, you will be prepared to guide and facilitate with confidence.

4. Gather any printed material and supplies you'll need for the session. If you're using technology, whether laptop, projector, audio system, or something else, be sure to rehearse. That way you can ensure an experience without glitches or embarrassment.

How to Lead a Discussion Group or Class

5. If someone in the group is sick or has a personal emergency, be sure to call, send a note or email, or visit in person. You might want to appoint a personal care team or committee who will do this for you and the group. This kind of pastoral care for one another can help foster a spiritual dynamic in the group that has a lasting impact in the personal lives of the people in the class.

6. In order to foster participation, be sure to ask people in advance to open or close in prayer, lead the singing, share a testimony, or be in charge of an activity. While there are some appropriate times for spontaneity, advance planning helps the sessions go much more smoothly.

DURING THE SESSION

1. Be in the room early so you are there as people arrive. It's important to start on time and end on time.
2. Open and close with prayer.
3. Try to lead in such a way that everyone in the group participates. You might need to encourage some to talk, while others you might ask to talk a little less in order for the others to participate more.
4. Make sure nobody is criticized for the way he or she answers a question, and no one should be coerced to share something personal.
5. Balance the discussion with regard to heavy and light, deep and superficial, practical and spiritual, professional and personal. You don't want it to be lopsided in any way.
6. Consider building some variety in the way you conduct the group. For instance, do some of the questions with the whole group, but sometimes form smaller groups of three or four people to discuss the questions and then report back to the

How to Lead a Discussion Group or Class

larger group. Some of the issues could easily become writing assignments, research projects, or class presentations.

7. If questions come up and you don't know the answers, simply be honest and acknowledge you don't have the answer at this time. Be sure to tell the group that you'll get that answer for the next session, and then follow up on it.

One Anothers of the New Testament

Love one another, for love comes from God.
Everyone who loves has been born of God and knows God.

1ˢᵀ JOHN 4:7–8

John 13:14	Wash one another's feet
John 13:34	Love one another
Romans 2:1	Don't judge one another
Romans 12:10	Be devoted to one another
Romans 12:10	Honor one another
Romans 12:16	Be in agreement with each other
Romans 14:13	Don't criticize each other
Romans 14:19	Build each other up
Romans 15:5	Live in harmony with each other
Romans 15:7	Accept one another
Romans 15:14	Teach each other
Romans 16:16	Greet one another with a holy kiss
1 Corinthians 11:33	Wait for one another
1 Corinthians 12:25	Be concerned for each other
Galatians 5:13	Serve one another

One Anothers of the New Testament

Galatians 5:15	Don't bite and devour each other
Galatians 5:26	Don't envy one another
Galatians 6:2	Carry each other's burdens
Ephesians 4:32	Be kind & compassionate to one another
Ephesians 4:32	Forgive each other
Ephesians 5:19	Speak to each other in psalms, hymns, and spiritual songs
Ephesians 5:21	Submit to one another
Philippians 2:3	Consider others better than yourselves
Colossians 3:9	Don't lie to each other
Colossians 3:13	Bear with one another
1 Thessalonians 4:18	Encourage each other
1 Thessalonians 5:11	Build each other up
1 Thessalonians 5:13	Live in peace with each other
1 Thessalonians 5:15	Pursue what is good for one another
Hebrews 10:24	Spur one another on toward love and good works
James 5:9	Don't complain about each other
James 5:16	Pray for each other
James 5:16	Confess your sins to one another
1 Peter 4:9	Be hospitable to one another
1 Peter 5:5	Humility toward one another
1 John 1:7	Fellowship with one another

About the Author

PAUL LINZEY TEACHES SPIRITUAL Formation and Practical Ministry at Called College in Carlinville, IL.

He was a pastor before becoming an Army chaplain. After retiring from the military in 2015 at the rank of Colonel, he and his wife planted Friendship Church, which is in Mulberry, FL, and then he taught full-time at Southeastern University in Lakeland, FL, where he developed the Creative Writing program, taught practical ministry classes, and served as a mentor in their Doctor of Ministry program.

When he became the Protestant pastor at the United States Naval Academy, in a sense he was *returning to the Blue Side* and coming full circle because he grew up in a Navy family. His father and brother were Navy chaplains, and one of his sons is currently a Navy chaplain. His other two sons are Army officers.

Linzey is an award-winning author who has written articles for religious and military magazines. He was a contributing writer and editor for Life Publisher's *The Warriors Bible* in 2014. In 2019 he self-published a book called *WisdomBuilt: Biblical Principles of Marriage*. His second book, released in 2020, has a foreword by Dr. Richard Blackaby and is titled *Safest Place in Iraq*. The book focuses on his experience as a military chaplain in Iraq during the war. His third book, *Military Ministry: Chaplains in the Twenty-First Century*, was co-written with Dr. Keith Travis, professor of practical ministry and chaplaincy at Liberty University. The foreword was written by Dr. Jeff Iorg, president of Gateway Seminary.

About the Author

His books are being used in several colleges and seminaries in the United States, as well as in many churches.

Linzey completed the Bachelor of Arts in Religious Studies at Vanguard University in Costa Mesa, CA. Graduate degrees include the Master of Divinity from Fuller Theological Seminary, the Doctor of Ministry at Gordon-Conwell Theological Seminary, and an MFA in Creative Writing at the University of Tampa. He has been a featured speaker at churches, marriage and family seminars, writers conferences and workshops, men's retreats, military events, and universities.

In addition to teaching at Called College, he is part of a chaplain team that has been asked to train chaplains for the Ukrainian military at a seminary in Ukraine. Throughout his adult life, whether serving in a church, the military, or the university, he has been involved in small group ministries, pastoral care, and lay leadership training.

Interests include music, digital photography, movies and theater, sports, travel, and family. He and his wife have three sons and ten grandchildren. He is a member of the North American Butterfly Association, and with his wife, maintains a registered butterfly garden.

His theme scripture is First Thessalonians 2:8, *We loved you so much that we were willing to share with you not only the gospel of God but our lives as well, because you had become so dear to us.* Linzey's website/blog is https://paullinzey.com. In addition, he can be found on Facebook and LinkedIn.

Books by Paul E. Linzey

Butterfly Believers
A WisdomBuilt Marriage
Safest Place in Iraq
Military Ministry

And by Linda S. Linzey, Ph.D.
Digging Deeper in First Corinthians

. . . .

Find out more about the Linzeys writings at

https://wisdombuilt.org
or at
https://paullinzey.com

The Music and Ministry of Eddie Espinosa

EDDIE ESPINOSA IS A minister, educator, counselor, musician, worship leader, composer, producer, song writer, and recording artist. In the early 1970s, he ministered in the Maranatha bands during the Jesus People revival and has been a worship leader with the Vineyard Movement for over 20 years. Twelve of those years he also served as a pastor.

He pastored the Vineyard's Spanish speaking congregation for four of those years, and led worship for the Promise Keepers Men's Conferences during the '95 and '96 season. He served on a team of advisors to help plan for the following season.

Eddie has composed many worship songs, including *You Are The Mighty King, Change My Heart, Oh God*, and *Con Mis Labios*. He has participated in countless worship recordings. He had the privilege of leading worship and teaching on the subject of worship not only in the U.S. and Canada, but also in England, Scotland, Ireland, South Africa, Australia, Germany, South Korea, Mexico, Honduras, Costa Rica, Colombia, and Chile. He also contributed to Zondervan's *Worship Bible Commentary*.

Espinosa completed two Masters Degrees, one in School Counseling, the other in School Administration. He retired from public education after thirty-five years experience in teaching, counseling and administration.

The Music and Ministry of Eddie Espinosa

His heart's desire is to see Psalm 67:3-4 come to pass: *May the peoples praise you, God; may all the peoples praise you. May the nations be glad and sing for joy.*

His passion for the Lord is evident in his music and worship leading. His goals are always the same, regardless of the size of congregation: to lead people into the presence of God, and that every participant will have an increased passion and love for the Savior.

Eddie is currently working on a new recording project that will be an anthology of classic songs combined with new songs. He is devoting more time to his family, as well as to mentor and coach worship leaders and songwriters. In the middle of all this, he is composing new music, writing a book, and enjoying a new sense of inspiration about what God is doing in the world today.

Bibliography

Ashworth, Hilaire. "Butterflies Warming Up." *Lewis Ginter Botanical Garden*, September 30, 2015. https://www.lewisginter.org/butterflieswarming-up/#:~:text=Butterflies%20are%20 cold%20blooded%20(ectothermic,fly %2C%20also%20known%20as%20thermoregulation.

Beaton, Caroline. "The Majority of People Are Not Introverts or Extroverts." *Psychology Today*, October 6, 2017. https://www.psychologytoday.com /us/ blog/the-gen-y-guide/201710/the-majority-people-are-not-introverts-or-extroverts.

Breyer, Melissa. "8 Spectacular Caterpillars That Look Like Snakes." *Treehugger*, August 6, 2020. https:// www.treehugger.com/spectacular-caterpillars-look-snakes-4859218.

Britannica, T. Editors of Encyclopaedia. "Caterpillar." *Encyclopedia Britannica*, September 22, 2021. https://www.britannica.com/science/ caterpillar."Metamorphosis." *Encyclopedia Britannica*, February 4, 2020.

Brown, Colin, ed. *The New International Dictionary of New Testament Theology*. Grand Rapids: Zondervan, 1981.

Bruce, F. F. *The Epistles to the Colossians, to Philemon, and to the Ephesians*. The New International Commentary on the New Testament. Grand Rapids: Eerdmans, 1984.

Burris, Judy, and Wayne Richards. *The Life Cycles of Butterflies*. Adams: Storey Publishing, 2006.

"Butterfly Life Cycle." *Wisconsin Pollinators*, Accessed May 14, 2022.

———. "Butterfly Life Cycle: Egg." https://wisconsinpollinators.com/BU/BA_ ButterflyEggs.aspx

———. "Butterfly Life Cycle: Chrysalis." https://wisconsinpollinators.com/ BU/BA_ButterflyChrysalis.aspx

———. "Butterfly Life Cycle: Metamorphosis." https://wisconsinpollinators. com/BU/BA_ButterflyMetamorphosis.aspx

Carle, Eric. *The Very Hungry Caterpillar*. New York: World Publishing, 1969. YouTube, March 20, 2021. https://www.youtube.com/watch?v=eXHScp0_ Vv8.

Carter, David. *Butterflies and Moths*. London: Doring Kindersley, 2002.

Bibliography

Casanowicz, I.M. "Parallelism in Hebrew Poetry." *Jewish Encyclopedia*. Accessed October, 27, 2023. https://jewishencyclopedia.com/articles/11902-parallelism-in-hebrew-poetry.

Chole, Alicia Britt. *Anonymous*. Nashville: Integrity, 2006.

Clarke, Cyril, Philip Macdonald Sheppard, and V. Scali. "All-female broods in the butterfly Hypolimnas bolina (L.)." *The Royal Society Publishing*, 29 April 1975. https://royalsocietypublishing.org/doi/ 10.1098/rspb.1975.0038.

"CPR—adult and child after onset of puberty." *MedlinePlus*. Accessed May 15, 2022. https:// medlineplus.gov/ency/article/000013. htm#:~:text=Time%20is%20very%20important%20when,4%20to%20 6%20minutes%20later.

Culin, J. "Lepidopteran." *Encyclopedia Britannica*, January 12, 2018. https:// www.britannica.com/animal/ lepidopteran. https://www.britannica.com/ animal/ lepidopteran/Form-and-function#ref135152.

D'Angelo, Kristen. "The Butterfly Dimension: Caterpillar." *Fund the White Butterfly*. Accessed May 16, 2022. https://thewhitebutterflyfund.com/ butterfly/butterflies/#:~:text=In%20fact%2C%20a%20typical%20 caterpillar,baby%20becoming%20a%203%2C000%20lb.

"Gestation Period For Cows & All Other Mammals." *Beef 2 Live*, May 10, 2022. https://beef2live.com/story-gestation-period-cows-mammals-0-109436.

Hadley, Debbie. "Insect Anatomy: The Parts of a Caterpillar." *ThoughtCo*, Aug. 25, 2020, https:// www.thoughtco.com/parts-of-a-caterpillar-1968482.

Holland, W. J. *The Butterfly Book*. New York: Doubleday, 1905.

Holt, Holly. "Nectar and pollen fuel pollinator life." *Penn State College of Agricultural Sciences*, Department of Entomology. https://ento.psu.edu/ research/ centers /pollinators/resources-and-outreach/disappearing-pollinators/nutrition. Accessed June 3, 2022.

Houston, Elaine. "Introvert vs Extrovert: A Look at the Spectrum and Psychology." *PositivePsychology.com*. January 26, 2022. https://positivepsychology. com/ introversion-extroversion-spectrum/#:~:text=The %20 first%20 official%20random%20sample, the% 20United%20States%20general%20 population.

"How Much Does a Caterpillar Weigh?" *Study.com*. Accessed May 16, 2022. https://study.com/academy/answer/how-much-does-a-caterpillar-weigh. html.

Johnson, Steve. "Facts About Butterfly Eggs." *Sciencing*, November 2019.

"Karner Blue Butterfly." *The Nature Conservancy*, September 9, 2018. https:// www.nature. org/en-us/get-involved/how-to-help/animals-we-protect / karner-blue-butterfly/#:~: text=There%20are %20 two%20broods%20 each,10%2D15%20days%20of%20June.

Kelly. "How to Find Butterfly Eggs." *Joyful Butterfly*. Accessed May 13, 2022. https://www.joyful butterfly.com/find-butterfly-eggs/#:~:text=As%20 seen%20in%20 these%20 egg,on%20species%20 and%20 other%20 conditions.

Bibliography

———. "What Do Caterpillars Eat? Host Plants" *Joyful Butterfly*. Accessed May 12, 2022. https://www.joyfulbutterfly.com/what-do-caterpillars-eat/.

"Life Cycle." *Nature North*. Accessed May 13, 2022. http://www.naturenorth.com/butterfly/english/02%20Life%20Cycle.html#:~:text=The%20life%20cycle%20of%20a,the%20life%20cycle%20that%20grows.

———. http://www.naturenorth.com/butterfly/english/02%20Life%20Cycle.html#:~:text=Broods,as%203%20broods%20each%20year.

Linzey, Paul E. *Safest Place in Iraq*. Nashville: Morgan James, 2021.

———. *WisdomBuilt: Biblical Principles of Marriage*. Oviedo: EA, 2019.

Marcus, Ben. "Do Caterpillars Have Tongues?" *Illinois Science Council*, November 23, 2015 https://www.illinoisscience.org/2015/11/do-caterpillars-have-tongues/#:~:text=Caterpillars%20can%20taste%20sweet%2C%20salty,bears%2C%20and%20most%20other%20animals.

Martinus, Danial. "This cute little caterpillar has multiple heads. Sort of." *Mashable SE Asia*, July 22, 2020. https://sea.mashable.com/science/11614/this-cute-little-caterpillar-has-multiple-heads-sort-of.

Myres, Quinn. "The Behind-the-Scenes Story of 'He's On Fire!' in Nba Jam." *Sports*. Accessed May 14, 2022. https://melmagazine.com/en-us/story/hes-on-fire-nba-jam.

"NatureMapping Animal Facts: Monarch Butterfly." *Washington Nature Mapping Program*. Accessed May 25, 2022. http://naturemappingfoundation.org/natmap/facts/monarch_712.html.

Oswalt, John N. *The Book of Isaiah*. The New International Commentary on the Old Testament. Grand Rapids: Eerdmans, 1998.

Pavid, Katie. "Body snatchers: eaten alive by parasitic wasps." *Natural History Museum*. Accessed May 13, 2022. https://www.nhm.ac.uk/discover/body-snatchers-eaten-alive.html.

Piercy, Katie. "Caterpillar Breathing Explained (What Are Spiracles?)" *Meadowia*. Accessed May 15, 2022. https://meadowia.com/caterpillar-breathing-explained/.

Puiu, Tibi. "How Butterflies Gruesomely Transform into Butterflies." *ZME Science*. Accessed May 21, 2022. https://www.zmescience.com/ecology/animals-ecology/how-caterpillar-turn-butterfly-0534534/.

Rosenblatt, Lynn. "My Skin's Too Tight." *The Munching Caterpillar*. Accessed May 17, 2022. https://monarchbutterflyusa.com/monarch-life-cycle/the-munching—caterpillar/.

Roosevelt, Theodore. *Quotefancy*, #9. https://quotefancy.com/theodore-roosevelt-quotes. Accessed June 2, 2022.

Sanny, Loren C. *How to Spend a Day in Prayer*. Colorado Springs: NavPress, 1962

Simpson, J. A. and E. S. C. Weiner. *The Oxford English Dictionary*, volume 7. Oxford: Clarendon Press, 1991. Pages 967 (inhale) and 1037 (inspire).

South Seaville Camp Meeting of the United Methodist Churches of Greater New Jersey, Accessed May 11, 2022. https://southseavillecampmeeting.org/.

Bibliography

Sapkota, Anupama. "Inhalation Vs Exhalation- Definition, 15 Differences, Examples." *The Biology Notes*, January 20, 2022. https://thebiologynotes.com/ inhalation-vs-exhalation/#:~:text=Inhalation%20is%20a%20 part%20of,the%20relaxation%20of%20respiratory%20muscles.

"The Very Hungry Caterpillar." *Wikipedia*. Accessed May 16, 2022. https://en.wikipedia.org/wiki/The_Very_ Hungry_Caterpillar.

Vane-Wright, Dick. *Butterflies: A Complete Guide to Their Biology and Behavior*. Second edition. Ithaca: Comstock Publishing, 2015.

VanSomeren, Lindsay. "How do caterpillars turn into butterflies and moths through metamorphosis?" *Untamed Science*. Accessed May 13, 2022. https://untamedscience.com/biology/ecology/ ecology-articles/butterflies-metamorphosis/.

Wagner, C. Peter. *Your Church Can Grow: Seven Vital Signs of a Healthy Church*. Eugene: Wipf & Stock, 2011. Originally published by Gospel Light Publications in 1976.

"Warmer weather begets more butterfly broods." *NBC5*, Albany, NY, Aug 12, 2012. https://www.mynbc5. com/article/warmer-weather-begets-more-butterfly-broods/3304570.

Warren, Rick. *The Purpose Driven Church*. Grand Rapids: Zondervan, 1995.

"What Are Insects Like on the Inside? Vol. 7, No. 16." *Bug's Eye View*, June 29, 2021. Mississippi State University.

"What Is Our Spiritual Food?" *Got Questions*. Accessed May 16, 2022. https://www.gotquestions.org /spiritual-food.html.

Wigington, Patti. "The History of Butterfly Magic and Folklore." *Learn Religions*, February 09, 2019https: //www.learnreligions.com/butterfly-magic-and-folklore-2561631#:~:text= According%20to%20folklore%2C%20a%20 wish,meant%20a%20long%20stormy%20summer.

Wininger, J. D. *The Chrysalis of Christ: Transforming Your Life in Christ*. Unpublished.

Cooper: *Winning Through Words*, winningthroughwords.com, 2018.

"X-ray Vision." *Superhero Wiki*. https://superheroes. fandom.com/wiki/X-Ray_ Vision. Accessed June 4, 2022.

"X-ray Vision." *Wikipedia*, February 25, 2022. https://en.wikipedia.org/wiki/X-ray_vision.

Scripture Index

OLD TESTAMENT

Genesis
1:4–31	39
1:26–28	84, 119
2:7	36

Deuteronomy
8:3	45

Nehemiah
8:10	22

Psalms
13:1–2	72
34:8	49
51:10	109
67:3–4	132
103:1	117, 118
119:165	51

Proverbs
3:5–6	24
15:4	108

Isaiah
61:1–3	97, 98

Jeremiah
17:9	109
29:11	89

Daniel
3:25	95

NEW TESTAMENT

Matthew
4:1–4	45, 46
6:19–33	107
7:13–14	10
13:1–23	99, 100
16:24	16
22:19–22	120
24:13	62
28:18–20	101, 102

Mark
1:35	70
10:46–52	72

Luke
4:16–21	97, 98
8:38–39	85
14:28	16
17:11–19	72

Scripture Index

John
3:16	39
4:8, 31–32	46
4:24	49
5:1–5	72
9:1–7	72
10:9	11
11:1–3	72
13:14	126
13:34	126
20:22	36

Acts
2:42–47	65
10:34	39

Romans
1:29–32	111
2:1	126
8:28	88
12:1–2	xi, 13, 81, 85
12:10	126
12:16	126
14:12–19	55, 126
15:5–14	126
16:16	126

1 Corinthians
3:5–7	4
7:17–24	54, 85
9:19–27	100, 114
11:1	114
11:33	126
12:12, 20	9
12:25	126
13:11	105
14:1–4	46

2 Corinthians
3:18	19
4:16–18	88
5:17	85
12:20	111

Galatians
1:18—2:1	70
3:28	9
4:4	72
5:13–15	126, 127
5:16–23	56, 57, 111
5:24–25	111
5:26	127
6:2	127

Ephesians
1:22–23	41
4:12–13	72
4:14–16	116
4:20–24	67, 82
4:32	127
5:19	127
5:21	127
6:10–18	61, 62

Philippians
1:6	89
2:3	127
3:10–14	30
4:7	51
4:8	13
4:9	14

Colossians
1:18	41, 42
3:9	127
3:13	127
3:17	68

1 Thessalonians
2:8	129
4:18	127
5:11–15	127

1 Timothy
3:6	24
6:9	21

Scripture Index

2 Timothy
3:16   36
4:7–8   51, 52

Hebrews
5:11–14   104
10:24   127

James
1:2–4   19, 94
3:1   24
5:9   127
5:16   127

1 Peter
2:1–3   104
4:9   127
5:5   127
5:8   20, 21

2 Peter
1:3–4   6
3:18   xiii

1 John
1:7   127
4:4–8   39, 40

Revelation
3:14–16   27
3:20   11
3:21   28

www.ingramcontent.com/pod-product-compliance
Lightning Source LLC
Chambersburg PA
CBHW070910160426
43193CB00011B/1413